AMERICAN DOCTORAL DISSERTATIONS IN THE ROMANCE FIELD

1876-1926

BY

R. M. MERRILL, A.M.
INSTRUCTOR IN COLUMBIA UNIVERSITY

NEW YORK
COLUMBIA UNIVERSITY PRESS
1927

PREFACE

It seems fitting to publish this year a bibliography of American Doctoral Dissertations in the Romance field. In August, 1926, Johns Hopkins issued a list of its Doctors' Dissertations, 1876-1926. On November 30, 1926, Harvard printed a list of its Doctors of Philosophy and Doctors of Science, 1873-1926. The first American Ph. D. in Romance Languages was granted to Lucius Henry Buckingham, Harvard, 1876. This is, then, the jubilee year for American Romance Studies.

Prof. J. L. Gerig has edited a number of lists of American Doctoral Dissertations in Romance Languages, prefacing each list with a survey of the Romance Language Department in the respective institutions: Johns Hopkins', Romanic Review, July-September, 1917, pages 328-340; Harvard's, *ibid.*, January-March, 1919, pages 67-78; Yale's, *ibid.*, January-March, 1920, pages 70-75; Columbia's, *ibid.*, January-March, 1921, pages 73-79. Prof. Gerig has kindly entrusted me with the continuation and completion of these lists, — to be presented together with the titles of theses of other institutions, hitherto unlisted. I have collected 521 titles of Doctoral Theses from 30 American Universities and Colleges. I believe my list to be the first of its kind. It has been my aim to make this compilation complete and accurate; nevertheless, I shall welcome corrections and additions, and I shall embody them in a second edition.

In addition to the lists above mentioned, I have utilized the lists of American Modern Language Doctoral Dissertations, published every October

since 1922, in the Modern Language Journal; and
the annual lists of American Doctoral Dissertations, compiled by the Library of Congress, 1912-
1925, — the 1926 volume of these lists being still
in press. In the main, I have taken the L. C. lists
as my model; but, occasionally, it has seemed ap-
propriate to insert titles and data regarding them,
as these came to me through correspondence and
registers.

I have included some dissertations from other
departments, wherever I have felt that their sub-
jects would be useful to workers in the Romance
field.

This bibliography is arranged alphabetically,
according to the names of the recipients of the
Ph. D. degree. Following the name is the insti-
tution conferring the Ph. D. degree and its date.
Daggers, — of which there are 318 —, before the
candidates' names, indicate membership in the
M. L. A.; and their addresses can be found in the
yearly List of Members. An asterisk before the
title of the dissertation, denotes that it has not
been published. There are 183 unpublished theses.
I have taken 133 notations from L. C. lists. For
many titles, I have added the L. C. card no., which
will be useful for ordering cards directly from
the Library of Congress. Two indexes, a Romance
authors' index and a topical index, render the
desired titles readily accesible. There are 33
death notices.

The total of 521 dissertations is distributed as
follows: Columbia, 93; Harvard, 91; John Hopkins, 83; Chicago, 48; Wisconsin, 37; Pennsylvania, 36; Yale, 27; Cornell, 19; New York, 14;
Bryn Mawr, 12; California, 10; Princeton, 8; Illinois, 6; Stanford, 5; Radcliffe, 5; Minnesota, 4;
Catholic U. of A., 4; Iowa, 3; Colorado, 2; Michigan, 2; Smith, 2; Virginia, 2; Teachers College
(Columbia), 1; Catholic Sisters' College (Brook-

land, D. C.), 1; Boston, 1; Indiana, 1; Missouri, 1; Nebraska, 1; Syracuse, 1; Washington, 1.

The average number of dissertations a year for each period of ten years is here estimated: 1876-1886, 1; 1886-1896, 2; 1896-1906, 9; 1906-1916, 15; 1916-1926, 25.

I have used the following special abbreviations: A., America; comp. or compar., comparative; D., Department; H., Humanistic; l., leaf (in L. C. notations); L. C., Library of Congress; M. L. A., Modern Language Association; PMLA., Publications of M. L. A.; rev., review; R. or Rom., Romance or Romanic; Stab. tip., Printing house; stud., studies; U. or Univ., University.

I wish to thank the librarians and professors who have co-operated with me, in answer to my letters, in order to make this list comprehensive and accurate, and to ascertain which theses exist on a given subject. In many cases the theses are available for inter-library loans. In almost all cases, they can be consulted in the libraries of the respective institutions. In a few cases, the theses have been lost, and I have endeavored to specify this.

I am indebted to Prof. H. C. Lancaster for having suggested this bibliography, several years ago; to Prof. J. L. Gerig for permission and backing to continue his work in this field; to Prof. G. L. van Roosbroeck for advice and encouragement; to Miss I. G. Mudge for valuable advice in bibliographical matters; to the Columbia University Press for undertaking the publication.

R. M. MERRILL

Columbia Univ.,   Revised,
    Dec. 1, 1926   June 1, 1927

LIST

ACTON, HUL-CEE MARCUS (Wisconsin, 1926)
*The soldier in modern French drama. 197 p.

†ADAMS, EDWARD LARRABEE (Harvard, 1907)
*The formation of nouns and adjectives in Pro-
vençal by the addition of suffixes.* Pub. as
"Word formation in Provençal" in Univ. of
Mich. stud. Humanistic series, ii, New York,
1913. xvii, 607 p. 13-16919

ADAMS, NICHOLSON BARNEY (Columbia, 1922)
The romantic dramas of García Gutiérrez.
[New York] Instituto de las Españas en los
Estados Unidos [1922] 3 p. l., 9-149 p. 1l.
22-14456

ALDRICH, HELEN J. [Mrs. Frank Kleeberger]
(Colorado, 1909) *The three unities in French
drama from Corneille to Hugo.

ALEXANDER, LUTHER HERBERT (Columbia, 1911)
*Participial substantives of the -ata type in the
Romance languages, with special reference to
French.* ... New York, 1912. xii, 164 p. [Col.
Univ. stud. in Rom. philol. and lit. no. 12]
12-18842. [Deceased.]

†ALLEN, LOUIS (Chicago, 1922) *De l'hermite et
del jougleour, a thirteenth century "conte
pieux."* [ed.] Paris, Solsona, 1925. 8l. 25-21413

ALPERN, HYMAN (New York, 1925) *La tragedia
por los celos, comedia famosa de Don Guillén
de Castro y Bellvís.* Champion, Paris, 1926.
158 p.

†ALTROCCHI, RUDOLPH (Harvard, 1914) *Two old
Italian versions of the legend of Saint Alexius.* Parts pub. in the Romanic rev., 1915. vi,
p. 353-363; Mod. philol., 1925. 22; 337-352.

ANDERSON, FREDERICK (Yale, 1915) *The literary experience of the Agricola.

†ANDISON, JOHN GORDON (Columbia, 1923) The
affirmative particles in French. [Toronto],
Univ. of Toronto press, 1923. 3 p. l., 9-104 p.
24-3530

†ANIBAL, CLAUDE E. (Indiana, 1922) *A critical
text, with introd. of "El Arpa de David", by
Mira de Amescua; together with a dissertation on Lisardo, his pseudonym.

†ARMSTRONG, EDWARD COOKE (Johns Hopkins,
1897) Le Chevalier à l'épée. An old French
poem. Baltimore, 1900. 72 p.

†ARMSTRONG, HENRY HERBERT (Michigan, 1905)
Autobiographic elements in Latin inscriptions.
New York, London. The Macmillan Co., 1910.
286 p. [U. of Mich. stud. H. ser. iii] A10-735

†ARNOLD, HARRISON HEIKES (Harvard, 1926)
*Romance imperatives.

†ARVIN, NEIL COLE (Harvard, 1917) *The comé-
dies vaudevilles of Eugène Scribe.

†ATKIN, ERNEST GEORGE (Harvard, 1916) Villemain and the historical method. [Part expanded and pub. as "Villemain and French
classicism". Univ. Wis. stud. No. 20, 1924. p.
126-151.] [Stud. Members Dept. Rom. langs.]

†ATKINSON, GEOFFROY (Columbia, 1920) The ex-
traordinary voyage in French Literature before 1700... New York, Col. Univ. press, 1920.
xiii, 192 p. [Col. Univ. stud. in Romance philol.
and lit.] 21-311

†AUSTIN, HERBERT DOUGLAS (Johns Hopkins,
1911) Accredited citations in Ristoro d'Arezzo's
Composizione del mondo; a study of sources...
[Torino, Stab. tip. dottor G. Momo, 1913] 51 p.

[Pub. also in Studi medievali, vol. 4, p. 335-382] 14-3220

†BABCOCK, EARLE BROWNELL (Chicago, 1915) *A critical edition of the Advision of Christine de Pizan, Part iii. [No MS. in the Univ. of Chi. library.]

†BACON, GEORGE WILLIAM (Pennsylvania, 1903) Life and dramatic works of Dr. Juan Pérez de Montalván. Philadelphia, 1903. 46 p. 3-26667

BAILIFF, LAURENCE DEANE (Stanford, 1923) *Synalepha and hiatus in Spanish poetry. 112 p.

†BARNEY, WINFIELD SUPPLY (Syracuse, 1916) Corneille's comedies as a mirror of contemporary events and of the theories of French polite society in the first half of the seventeenth century... [Canaan, N. H., Press of C. O. Barney & Son, 1916] ix, 65 p. 17-18369

BARRANCO, MANUEL (Teachers College, Columbia, 1914) Mexico, its educational problems. Suggestions for their solution. New York, Teachers College, 1914. vii, 78 p. 16-14149

†BARROW, SARAH FIELD (Columbia, 1920) The medieval society romances. New York, Columbia Univ. press, 1924. 5 p. l., 141 [l.] p. [Half-title: Col. Univ. stud. in Eng. and compar. lit.] 24-21611

BARRY, Sister MARY FINBARR (Catholic Univ. of America, 1926)... The vocabulary of the moral-ascetical works of Saint Ambrose; a study in Latin lexicography... Washington, D. C. The Cath. Univ. of A., 1926. xiii, 287 p. [The Cath. Univ. of A. Patristic studies, vol. x] 26-17824

BARRY, Sister MARY INVIOLATA (Catholic Univ. of America, 1924) St. Augustine, the orator;

a study of the rhetorical qualities of St. Augustine's Sermones ad populum. Washington, D. C., The Catholic Univ. of America, 1924. xi, 261 p., 1l. [The Catholic Univ. of America. Patristic Studies. Vol. vi.] 24-18536

BARTLETT, HELEN (Bryn Mawr, 1896) *The metrical division of the Paris Psalter.* Baltimore, The Friedenwald co., 1986. 49 p. A19-44

†BAXTER, ARTHUR HENRY (Johns Hopkins, 1898) *The introduction of classical metres into Italian poetry and their development to the beginning of the nineteenth century.* Baltimore, J. Murphy co., 1901. 33 p. 3-5096

BEACH, ROBERT MILLS (Pennsylvania, 1907) *Was Fernando de Herrera a Greek Scholar? ...* Phila., [Univ. of Pa. publs. Series in Romanic langs. et lits., No. 2, 1908. 49 p.] 9-21290

†BEARDSLEY, WILFRED ATTWOOD (Columbia, 1917) *Infinitive construction in old Spanish...* New York, Columbia Univ. press, 1921. xiv, 279 p., 1l. [Half-title: Col. Univ. stud. in Romance philol. and lit.] 21-9382

BECKMANN, FREDERICH ERNST (Chicago, 1900) *Spanish influence on Eichendorff.* [No MS. in the Univ. of Chi. lib.]

†BERGERON, MAXIME L. (New York, 1914) *Syntax of Pierre Charron's "Traité de la sagesse" compared with that of Rabelais and Montaigne.*

†BERKOWITZ, HYMAN C. (Cornell, 1924) *Ramón de Mesonero Romanos; a study of his "costumbrista" essays.*

†BERNBAUM, ERNEST (Harvard, 1907) *Sentimental and domestic drama in England and France: its nature, its origin, and its history to the year 1750.* [About one-fourth pub., in revised form,

in chaps. 2, 3, 4, and 10 of "The drama of sensibility: a sketch of the history of English sentimental comedy and domestic tragedy, 1696-1780", Boston, Ginn, 1915. 8°. ix, 288 p.] [Harv. studies in Eng., 3.] 15-27986

BÉZIAT DE BORDES, ANDRÉ (Chicago, 1899) *Etude sur le dialecte de Balansun, Basses Pyrénées. I, Phonétique. [No Ms. in Univ. of Chi. library.] [Deceased, 1924.]

†BISHOP, MORRIS GILBERT (Cornell, 1926) *The plays of Jules Lemaître.

†BISSELL, CLIFFORD HERSHEY (California, 1925) *Conventions of the contemporary French bourgeois drama.

†BLONDHEIM, DAVID SIMON (John Hopkins, 1910) Contribution à la lexicographie française d'après des sources rabbiniques. Paris, 1910. 55 p. Reprinted fr. Romania, vol. xxxix. A11-1063

BLOSSOM, FREDERICK AUGUSTUS (Johns Hopkins, 1914) La composition de Salammbô d'après la correspondance de Flaubert (1857-1862) avec un essai de classement chronologique des lettres... Baltimore, The Johns Hopkins press, 1915. 54 p. 1l. Also, Paris, E. Champion, 1914. vii. 104 p. [An incomplete reprint from the Elliott monographs, No. 3, ix, 104 p.] 15-17209

BOECKER, ALEXANDER (New York, 1912) A probable Italian source of Shakespeare's "Julius Caesar"..... New York, 1913. viii, 130 p. 14-4949

DE BOER, JOSEPHINE MARIE (Johns Hopkins, 1925) *The life and works of Guillaume Colletet (1596-1659).

BONNOTTE, FERDINAND (Johns Hopkins, 1896) *Phonologie et morphologie du dialecte picard dans le Laonnais et le Soissonnais.

†BOURLAND, CAROLINE BROWN (Bryn Mawr, 1905) *Boccaccio and the Decameron in Castilian and Catalan literature.* New York, Paris, Mâcon, Protat Frères, 1905. 8ᵛᵒ, 233 p., 5 plates. [Reprint from "Revue hispanique", tome xii.] 6-7796

BOWEN, BENJAMIN LESTER (Johns Hopkins, 1888) *Contributions to periphrasis in the Romance languages.* [Deceased, 1920.]

†BOWEN, RAY PRESTON (Cornell, 1916) *The novels of Ferdinand Fabre, including an account of his life and a discussion of his position in literature.* Boston, R. G. Badger [1918] 138 p. 1l. [Half-title: Stud. in lit.] 20-89

†BOWMAN, EDGAR MILTON (Columbia, 1925) *The early novels of Paul Bourget.* New York, Carranza, 1925. 116 p. 25-22138

BRANDENBURG, GEORGE CLINTON (Wisconsin, 1915) *Psychological aspects of language...* [Baltimore, 1918] Cover-title, p. 313-332. ["Reprint from the Journal of educational psychology, vol. ix, no. 6. June, 1918".] 20-2742

BRAUER, HERMAN GUSTAV ADOLPH (Wisconsin, 1902) *The philosophy of Ernest Renan.* [Philol. and lit. series of the Bulletin of the Univ. of Wis., Madison, Vol. ii, no. 3, 1903. 176 p.] 5-34346

BREHAUT, ERNEST (Columbia, 1912) *An encyclopedist of the dark ages: Isidore of Seville...* New York, 1912. 2 p. l., 7-275 p. [Pub. also as Stud. in hist., econ., and public law, ed. by the Faculty of pol. science of Col. Univ. Vol. xlviii, no. I, whole no. 120.] 12-18646

†BRENNER, CLARENCE DIETZ (Princeton, 1926) *Themes from French history in eighteenth century French tragedy.* [In press.]

†BRINSMADE, CHAPIN (Yale, 1926) *Verse enjambement in Old Provençal poetry. ii, 202 p.

†BRONK, ISABELLE (Chicago, 1900) The "Poesies Diverses" of Antoine Furetière; a partial reprint from the edition of 1664. Ed. with introd., notes, and glossary. Baltimore, 1908. 113 p.

†BROOKS, JOHN (Wisconsin, 1924) *La gran comedia del mayor imposible de Lope de Vega Carpio. 430 p.

BROWN, FREDERIC WILLIS (Harvard, 1906) *An historical study of the preterite tense in Italian.

BROWN, IRVING HENRY (Columbia, 1921) Leconte de Lisle; a study of the man and his poetry. New York, Col. Univ. press, 1924. xiii p., 1l., 272 p. [Half-title: Col. Univ. stud. in Romance philol. and lit.] 24-19430

BROWNELL, GEORGE GRIFFIN (Johns Hopkins, 1904) The position of the attributive adjective in the Don Quixote. Paris, 1908. 35 p. [Reprinted from the Revue hispanique. Vol. xix, 20-50.] 13-22980

†BRUCE, HAROLD LAWTON (Yale, 1915) Voltaire on the English stage... Berkeley, Univ. of Calif. press [1918] cover-title, p. [I], 152. [Univ. of Calif. publs. in modern philol. v. 8. no. 1.] "This study is the revision of a thesis of the same title, submitted in 1915 to the faculty of the graduate school of Yale Univ., in candidacy for the degree of doctor of philosophy". Pref. ... A. 18-763

†BRUERTON, COURTNEY (Harvard, 1915) *Chapters in the history of the "comédie-vaudeville" from its origins to the present time.

†BRUNER, JAMES DOWDEN (Johns Hopkins, 1894) The phonology of the Pistojese Dialect. Balti-

more, 1894. vi, 88 p. [Reprinted from the PMLA, Vol. ix, no. 4.]

BRUNO, JOHN FAVATA (Columbia, 1915) *Rosmini's contribution to ethical philosophy...* New York. The Science press, 1916. iii, 54 p. [Archives of philos., ed. by F. J. E. Woodbridge, no. 6. February, 1916.] 16-14742

†BRUSH, HENRY RAYMOND (Chicago, 1911) *La bataille de trente, a Middle-French poem of the fourteenth century...* [ed.] *by Henry Raymond Brush...* Chicago, 1912. iv, 90 p. [Reprinted from Modern philol., vol. ix, no. 4, and vol. x, no. 1, 1912.] 13-7609

†BRUSH, MURRAY PEABODY (Johns Hopkins, 1898) [ed.] *The Isopo laurenziano, with notes and an introd., treating of the interrelation of Italian fable collections.* Columbus, 1899. viii, 186 p.

†BUCHANAN, MILTON ALEXANDER (Chicago, 1906) *Comedia famosa del esclavo del Demonio compuesta por el doctor Mira de Amescua* [Barcelona, 1612], *Ed. with an introd. and notes.* Baltimore, 1905. 144 p.

BUCKINGHAM, LUCIUS HENRY (Harvard, 1876) [Master, English High School, Boston, Mass., 1881-1885]. *That the Romance languages, in deriving from the Latin, followed tendencies to change, which the Latin already exhibited, is illustrated by the study of Romance verbal formations.* [Deceased, 1885.]

†BUFFUM, DOUGLAS LABAREE (Johns Hopkins, 1904) *Le roman de la violette; a study of the manuscripts and the original dialect.* Baltimore, J. Furst co., 1904. 84 p. 4-37069

†BULLOCK, WALTER LLEWELLYN (Harvard, 1923) *Characteristics of the sonnet in the first half of the Cinquecento.*

BURTON, JOHN MARVIN (Johns Hopkins, 1916) *Honoré de Balzac and his figures of speech...* Baltimore, The Johns Hopkins press, 1921. 30 p., 1l. ["An incomplete reprint from the Elliott monographs, no. 9 (i. e. no. 8)"] [Deceased, 1918.] 21-17822. [Also, Princeton & Paris, 1921. 4 p. l., 98 p.] 21-17821

†BUSSOM, THOMAS WAINWRIGHT (Minnesota, 1922) *The life and dramatic works of Pradon.* Paris, E. Champion, 1922. 194 p. 1l. 22-20875

BYRNE, EUGENE HUGH (Wisconsin, 1915) *Commercial contracts of the Genoese in the Syrian trade of the twelfth century.* [Cambridge, Mass., 1916] cover-title, [1] 128-170 p. ["Reprinted from the Quarterly journal of econ. vol. xxxi, November 1916".] 17-21391

†CABEEN, DAVID CLARK (Pennsylvania, 1923) *The African novels of Louis Bertrand: a phase of the renascence of national energy in France.* Philadelphia. Printed by Westbrook pub. co., 1922. 106 p. 23-6792

†CALCOTT, FRANK (Columbia, 1923) *The supernatural in early Spanish literature, studied in the works of the court of Alfonso X, el Sabio.* New York. Instituto de las Españas en los Estados Unidos, 1923. 154 p. 23-11223

†CALMAN, ALVIN ROSENBLATT (Columbia, 1922) *Ledru-Rollin and the second French republic.* New York, 1922. 2 p. l., 7-453 p. [Pub. also as Stud. in hist. econ. and pub, law. vol. ciii, no. 2, whole no. 234.] 23-1656

†CAMBIAIRE, CELESTIN PIERRE (Iowa, 1926) *The influence of Edgar Allan Poe in France.* [Revised and condensed. Pub. in Romanic review, xvii, Oct.-Dec., 1926. p. 319-337.]

†CAMERA, AMERIGO ULYSSES NICHOLAS (New

York, 1912) *Italian influences upon French comedy before Molière*. 80 p.

CANFIELD, DOROTHEA FRANCES [Mrs. John Redwood Fisher] (Columbia, 1904) *Corneille and Racine in England. A study of the English translations of the two Corneilles and Racine with special reference to their presentation on the English stage.* New York. The Columbia Univ. press, 1904. xiii, 295 p. A11-48A.

†CARNAHAN, DAVID HOBART (Yale, 1905) *The prologue in the Old French and Provençal mystery.* New Haven, Conn., The Tuttle, Morehouse & Taylor co., 1905. 200 p. 5-27159

CARTER, CHARLES HENRY (Harvard, 1904) *Ipomedon: a study of the poem and of the questions raised thereby.* Pub. in part as "Ipomedon, an illustration of Romance origin", in Haverford Essays, Haverford, Pa., 1909. p. 235-270. [Dept. of Eng. lit.]

†CASTILLO, CARLOS (Chicago, 1923) *En la vida todo es verdad, y todo mentira, by D. Pedro Calderón de la Barca: an edition from the autograph with introd. and notes.*

†CATTELL, JAMES LLEWELLYN (Wisconsin, 1913) *Le ménage à trois in French farce comedy.*

†CERF, BARRY H. (Harvard, 1908) *A classification of the manuscripts of Ogier le Danois.* Published, condensed, in PMLA., 1908. xxiii, p. 545-555.

†CHANDLER, FRANK WADLEIGH (Columbia, 1899) *Romances of roguery. Part. I., The picaresque novel in Spain.* New York, Col. Univ. press, 1899. ix, 483 p. [D. compar. lit.] A11-50

†CHENERY, WINTHROP HOLT (Harvard, 1904) *Object pronouns in dependent clauses: a study in*

Old Spanish word order. Pub. with omissions, in PMLA., 1905. xx, p. 1-151.

CHESKIS, JOSEPH ISRAEL (Harvard, 1917) *Philological studies in Judaeo-Spanish.* Results pub. as "Old French dancier", Mod. philol., 1917. XIV: 175-176; "Ladino Meldar and Alumnar," Rom. rev., 1918. IX: 111-112.

CHILD, JOHN ALLAN (Johns Hopkins, 1917) **The subjunctive in the Decameron: primary and concessive clauses.*

†CHURCHMAN, PHILIP HUDSON (Harvard, 1908) *Byron and the Spanish peninsula.* Portions pub. as "Espronceda's Blanca de Borbón", in the Revue hispanique, 1907. xvii, p. 549-777, pl. 3-6; "Lord Byron's experiences in the Spannish peninsula in 1809", in the Bulletin hispanique, 1909. xi, p. 55-95, 125-171; "Byron and Espronceda", in the Revue hispanique, 1909. xx, p. 5-210; and "The beginnings of Byronism in Spain", ibid., 1910. xxiii, p. 333-410.

CIPRIANI, LISI CECILIA (Chicago, 1898) **Introduction to a critical edition of Gui de Bourgogne.* [No MS. in Univ. of Chi. library.]

†CLARK, ALEXANDER FREDERICH BRUCE (Harvard, 1916) *Boileau in England, with some notes on the influence of the other French critics, 1660-1830.* Modified, enlarged, and pub. as "Boileau and the French classical critics in England (1660-1830)", Paris, E. Champion, 1925. p. xviii, 534 [Bibliothèque de la Revue de Littérature comparée, 19.] 26-16444

CLARK, JOHN TAGGART (Harvard, 1901) *An examination of the development of medial consonants in Italian, with special reference to the question of accent influence.* Results pub. in part in Romania, 1903. xxxii, p. 593-596; 1904. xxxiii, p. 246-248; 1905. xxxiv, p. 66-86.

†CLARK, THATCHER (Harvard, 1902) *Long unaccented final e, in Latin, does not phonetically become i, in Italian.*

CLARKE, JOHN ALFRED (Columbia, 1923) *Le laie Bible, a poem of the fourteenth century, with introduction, notes, and glossary.* New York, Col. Univ. press, 1923. v, 150 p. 1l. [Pub. also in the series Col. Univ. stud. in Romance philol., and lit.] 24-5127

†CLÉMENT, NEMOURS HONORÉ (Chicago, 1923) *The five books of Rabelais, considered as a romance.*

†COESTER, ALFRED LESTER (Harvard, 1906) *Compression in the Poema del Cid.* Pub. in part in the Revue hispanique, 1906. xv, p. 98-211.

COHEN, HELEN LOUISE (Columbia, 1914) *The ballade...* New York, Col. Univ. press, 1915. xix, 398 p. [Col. Univ. stud. in Eng. and compar. lit.] 15-16409

COLBERT, *Sister* MARY COLMKILLE (Catholic U. of America, 1923) *The syntax of the De Civitate Dei of St. Augustine.* Washington, D. C., The Catholic Univ. of America, 1923. x, 105 p. 1l. [The Cath. Univ. of A. Patristic studies. Vol. iv.] 24-5342

†COLEMAN, ALGERNON (Johns Hopkins, 1913) *Flaubert's literary development in the light of his Mémoires d'un fou, Novembre and Éducation sentimentale (version of 1845)...* Baltimore, The Johns Hopkins press, 1915. 31 [1] p. [Dissertation issue is reprint of part I, chap. I only.] ["An incomplete reprint from the Elliott monographs, no. 1.] [Also, Balto. & Paris, E. Champion, 1914, xv, 154 p.] 15-17317 & 15-12286

COLIN, THÉRÈSE FORNACHON (Pennsylvania,

1897) *Archaisms in Modern French. 150 p.
[Deceased.]

†COMFORT, WILLIAM WISTAR (Harvard, 1902) *The
development of the character types in the
French chansons de geste. PMLA., 1906. xxi,
p. 279-434.

†CONRAD, ELISABETH (Wisconsin, 1919) *Evolution of French criticism of the social drama
of Ibsen from 1890-1906. 90 p.

†CONSTANS, ANTONY (Harvard, 1926) *Recher-
ches sur Louis de Boissy (1694-1758).

†COOL, CHARLES DEAN (Wisconsin, 1909) *French
literature in American magazines, prior to
1830.

†CORLEY, AMES HAVEN (Yale, 1914)... Word-
play in the Don Quixote... New York [etc.],
1917. 2 p. l., 49 p. ["Extrait de la Revue
hispanique, 1917. tome xl."] 18-6681

†CORNISH, [MRS.] BEATRICE QUIJADA (California,
1925) *Francisco Navarro Villoslada.

CORWIN, EDWARD SAMUEL (Pennsylvania, 1905)
French policy and the American alliance of
1778... Princeton, Princeton Univ. press, 1916.
ix, 430 p., 1l. 17-1004

†COWPER, FREDERICK AUGUSTUS GRANT (Chicago,
1920) The sources, date and style of "Ille et
Galeron" by Gautier d'Arras. [Chicago, 1922]
22 p. "Private edition, distributed by the Univ.
of Chicago libraries". "Reprinted from Modern philology, vol. xviii, no. ii, March, 1921,
and vol. xx, no. i, August, 1922". 22-21074

CRABB, WILSON DEANE (Chicago, 1897) Culture
history in the chanson de geste, "Aymeri de
Narbonne", Chicago, 1897. xxvi, 95 p.

†CRANE, RONALD SALMON (Pennsylvania, 1911)

The vogue of medieval chivalric romance during the English renaissance. Menasha, Wis. George Banta publishing company, 1919. 2 p.l., 53 p. [Abstract of thesis.] 20-2346

†CRAWFORD, JAMES PYLE WICKERSHAM (Pennsylvania, 1906) *The life and works of Cristóbal Suárez de Figueroa.* [U. of Pa. publs. Series in Romanic langs. and lits., No. 1, 1907. 159 p.] 8-259

CRAWFORD, LUCY SHEPARD (Cornell, 1923) *The Philosophy of Émile Boutroux as representative of French idealism in the nineteenth century* [Charlottesville, Va., Surber-Arundale co.] 1924. 4 p. l., 153 p. [Pub. as Cornell stud. in philos. no. 16.] 25-10711

†CRAWFORD, MARY SINCLAIR (Pennsylvania, 1923) *Life of Saint Nicholas by Wace.* [U. of Pa. publs. Series in Romanic langs. and lits., No. 12, 1924. 115 p.]

CRAWFORD, WILLIAM REX (Pennsylvania, 1926) *The freeman's morals. A critique of the philosophy of Remy de Gourmont.* Pub. Philadelphia, 1926. 50 p. [D. of philos.] 26-15762

CRESSON, WILLIAM PENN (Columbia, 1922) *The Holy alliance; the European background of the Monroe Doctrine.* New York [etc.], Oxford Univ. press, 1922. 3 p. l., 147 p. [Pub. also in Publs. of the Carnegie endowment for international peace; Division of international law.] 23-1655

CRITCHLOW, F. L. (Johns Hopkins, 1903) *On the forms of betrothal and wedding ceremonies in the Old-French romans d'aventure.* Chicago, 1905. 41 p. [Reprinted from Modern philology. vol. ii, p. 497-537.] 5-38800

†CROOKS, ESTHER JOSEPHINE (Johns Hopkins, 1923) *The influence of Cervantes in France*

during the first half of the seventeenth century, with special reference to Guérin de Bouscal and a critical edition of his Gouvernement de Sanche Pansa.

CRU, ROBERT LOYALTY (Columbia, 1913) *Diderot as a disciple of English thought.* New York, Columbia Univ. press, 1913. xii, 500 p. [Col. Univ. stud. in Romance philol. and lit.] 13-33956

†CUMMINGS, HUBERTIS MAURICE (Princeton, 1914) *The indebtedness of Chaucer's works to the Italian works of Boccaccio (a review and summary)...* Menasha, Wis., George Banta publishing company, 1916. 4 p. l., 202 p. [University of Cincinnati stud., vol. X (part 2), Cincinnati, Ohio, 1916.] 17-1794

CURDY, ALBERT EUGENE (Johns Hopkins, 1902) [ed.] *La folie Tristran, an Anglo-Norman poem.* Part I. Baltimore, 1903. 40 p. [Printed dissertation issue does not contain text of poem.] 4-37068

CURTIS, EUGENE NEWTON (Columbia, 1917) *The French Assembly of 1848 and American constitutional doctrines...* New York, 1917. 2 p. l., 7-359 p. [Pub. also as Stud. in hist., econ., and pub. law, ed. by the Faculty of pol. science of Col. Univ. vol. lxxix, no. 2. whole no. 184.] 18-7525

†CUSHING, MARY GERTRUDE (Columbia, 1908) *Pierre Le Tourneur.* New York, The Columbia Univ. press, 1908. 12mo, xi, 317 p. 8-30946

CUSHING, MAX PEARSON (Columbia, 1914) *Baron d'Holbach, a study of eighteenth century radicalism in France.* New York, 1914. iii p, 1l., 108 p. 1l. 15-3711

†DALE, GEORGE IRVING (Cornell, 1917) *The

Moors in the Spanish drama of the Golden Age.

†DANA, HENRY WADSWORTH LONGFELLOW (Harvard, 1910) *Mediaeval visions of the other world.* [Dept. of compar. lit.]

†DARGAN, EDWIN PRESTON (Johns Hopkins, 1906) *The aesthetic doctrine of Montesquieu, its application in his writings.* Baltimore, J. Furst co., 1907. 203 p. 7-40878

DAVIDSON, GEORGE DINGUID (Virginia, 1905) *The style of Adenet Le Roi studied in 'Berte' and 'Cleomades'.*

†DAWSON, JOHN CHARLES (Columbia, 1921) *Toulouse in the renaissance: the Floral games; university and student life; Etienne Dolet (1532-1534)... Pt. I. The Floral games of Toulouse (les Jeux floraux)...* New York, Columbia Univ. press, 1921. xiv, 87, [1] p. [Pub. also in Columbia Univ. stud. in Romance philol. and lit.] 22-19642

DEDECEK, V. L. (Pennsylvania, 1925) *Etude littéraire et linguistique de li Hystori de Julius Cesar de Jehan de Tuim.* Phila. [U. of Pa. Series in Romanic langs. and lits. no. 13, 1926. 132 p.] [Printed in France.]

DEFERRARI, HARRY (Pennsylvania, 1926) *The sentimental Moor in Spanish Literature.* Philadelphia, [U. of P. Series in Romanic langs. and lits., no. 17.] [In press.]

†DE FOREST, JOHN BELLOWS (Yale, 1915)... *Old French borrowed words in the Old Spanish of the twelfth and thirteenth centuries, with special reference to the Cid, Berceo's poems, the Alexandre and Fernán González...* [In the Romanic review. New York, 1916. vol. vii, no. 4, p. 369-413.] 19-16238

†DEGELER, ALIDA (Wisconsin, 1917) *The devil: a dramatic figure in the religious drama of Mediaeval France. [No MS. in U. of Wis. lib.]

DE HAAN, FONGER (Johns Hopkins, 1895) An outline of the history of the novela picaresca in Spain. The Hague, M. Nijhoff, 1903. xii, 125 p. 4-29849

DELAMARRE, L. (New York, 1905) *Tacite et la littérature française. [Dept. of Latin.]

†DE VRIES, LOUIS PETER (Wisconsin, 1913) *A comparison of the realism in the modern French novel and drama.

DEXTER, ELSIE FORSYTHE (Wisconsin, 1926, Sum. Sess.) *Sources of the cantigas of Alfonso el Sabio. 193 p.

†DEY, WILLIAM MORTON (Harvard, 1906) The history of the prefix "por-" in Old French. [Pub. somewhat rearranged, as "The Latin prefix pro in French" in Stud. in Philol., Univ. of N. C., 1915. xii, p. 135-182.]

†DICKMAN, ADOLPHE JACQUES (Iowa, 1925) Le rôle du surnaturel dans les chansons de geste. Pub. Iowa City, State U. of Iowa, le 27 mai 1925. 208 p. Also, Paris, E. Champion, 1926. xii, 208 p. 26-18431

DI SANTO, SALADINO VINCENZO (Pennsylvania, 1916) *La fortuna del Principe del Machiavelli in Ispagna. 95 p. [Deceased.]

†DITCHY, JAY KARL (Johns Hopkins, 1924) La mer dans l'œuvre littéraire de Victor Hugo. Baltimore, 1925. 58 p. A part only. [Revised. Paris, Société d'édition. "Les Belles-Lettres" (95 Boul. Raspail) 1925. 238 p.] 26-5836

†DONDO, MATHURIN MARIUS (Columbia, 1922) Vers libre a logical development of French

verse. Paris, E. Champion, 1922. 87 p. 1l.
22-18160 Revised.

†DOTY, GEORGE LEWIS (Illinois, 1925) **Juan de
Zabalete, "El día de fiesta por la mañana".* A
critical annotated edition.

†DOWNER, CHARLES ALFRED (Columbia, 1901)
Frédéric Mistral, poet and leader in Provence.
New York, The Columbia Univ. press, 1901.
12ᵐᵒ, x, 267 p. HCL 17-3076

†DOXSEE, CARLL WHITMAN (Princeton, 1916)
Hume's relation to Malebranche... [Boston,
1916] i p. l., [1] 692-710 p. "Reprinted from
the Philosophical review, vol. xxv, no. 5...
September, 1916." 16-22961

†DULAC, VICTOR (Johns Hopkins, 1920) **L'esthétique littéraire de Voltaire.*

†DUNN, JOHN JOSEPH (Yale, 1898) **Vocabulary
to the Orlando Furioso of Ariosto, cantos 1-3.*

†DUTTON, GEORGE BURWELL (Harvard, 1910)
*Thomas Rymer and Aristotelian formalism in
English literary criticism, 1650-1700.* Por-
tions revised, enlarged, and pub. as "The
French Aristotelian formalists and Thomas
Rymer" in PMLA, 1914. xxix: 152-188; and
'Dramatic fashions illustrated in six old
plays', in Journal Eng. and Ger. philol., 1914.
xiii: 398-417. [Dept. Eng. lit.]

†EASTER, DE LA WARR BENJAMIN (Johns Hopkins, 1905) *A study of the magic elements in
the romans d'aventure and the romans bretons.* Part I. Baltimore, 1906. 56 p. [Printed
dissertation issue contains part I.] 6-37892

†EDDY, HELEN MAY (Iowa, 1925) **"The French
element in Thorndike's 'The Teacher's Work
Book'."*

†EDGERLY, CLIFTON TISDALE (Yale, 1918) **A vo-

cabulary of the Siete Partidas of Alfonso X.
vii, 277 p.

EDWARDS, BATEMAN (Princeton, 1924) *A classification of the Manuscripts of Gui de Cambrai's Vengement Alixandre...* Princeton and Paris, 1926. 51 p. [Elliott monographs, no. 20.]

†ENGLISH, JAMES HENRY (Columbia, 1926) *The alternation of "h" and "f" in Old Spanish.* New York, Instituto de las Españas, 1926. 162 p. 26-14512

†ESPINOSA, AURELIO MACEDONIO (Chicago, 1909) *Studies in New Mexican Spanish.* I, Brussels and Chicago, 1909. 115 p. A11-1172

ETTARI, FRANCESCO (Columbia, 1918) *El giardeno of Marino Jonata, Agnonese; an Italian poem of the fifteenth century.* New York, Columbia Univ. press, 1924. 2 p. l., 83, [1] p. [Out of print.] [Half-title: Columbia Univ. stud. in Romance philol. and lit.] [Deceased.] 24-20164.

EVELETH, F. W. (New York, 1899) **La novela picaresca and its influence upon subsequent literature.*

†EVERS, HELEN MARGARET (Bryn Mawr, 1905) *Critical edition of the Discours de la Vie de Pierre de Ronsard, par Claude Binet.* Philadelphia, The John C. Winston Co., 1905. 8ᵛᵒ, iv, 190 p. [Reprint from Bryn Mawr College monograph series, vol. ii.]

†FAHNESTOCK, EDITH (Bryn Mawr, 1915) *A study of the sources and composition of the old French Lai d'Haveloc.* Jamaica, New York [etc.], The Marion press, 1915. 3 p. l., [5] 138 p., 1l. 16-5894

†FANSLER, DEAN SPRUILL (Columbia, 1913) *Chaucer and the Roman de la Rose...* New

York, Columbia Univ. press, 1914. 6 p. l.,
269 p., 1l. [Columbia Univ. stud. in Eng. and
comp. lit. (v. 8).] 14-5538

†FARNHAM, CARRIE EVANGELINE (Columbia,
1921) *American travellers in Spain. The Spanish inns, 1776-1867...* New York, Columbia
Univ. press, 1921. v, 58 p. 21-10180

†FARNSWORTH, WILLIAM OLIVER (Columbia, 1913)
*Uncle and nephew in the Old French chansons
de geste: a study in the survival of matriar-
chy...* New York, Columbia Univ. press, 1913.
xii, 268 p. [Pub. also as Col. Univ. stud. in
Romance philol. and lit.] 13-17174

FAY, EDWARD ALLEN (Johns Hopkins, 1881)
**On the conditional relations in the Romance
Languages*. [Deceased, 1923.]

†FAY, PERCIVAL BRADSHAW (Johns Hopkins, 1912)
*Elliptical partitiv usage in affirmativ clauses
in French prose of the fourteenth, fifteenth,
and sixteenth centuries...* Paris, H. Champion, 1912. viii, 87, [1] p. 12-32064

†FERARU, LEON (Columbia, 1927) **Studies in
Roumanian poetry*. [Ed. R. M. M. In process
of revision.]

†FERGUSON, JOHN DE LANCY (Columbia, 1916)
American literature in Spain... New York,
Columbia Univ. press, 1916. xiii, 267 p. 1l.
[Columbia Univ. stud. in Eng. and comp. lit.]
17-6371

†FESS, GILBERT MALCOLM (Pennsylvania, 1924)
*The correspondence of physical and material
factors with character in Balzac.* 1924. vi, 108p.
[Univ. of Pa. publs. Series in Rom. langs. and
lits. no. 10.] 24-25333

FIALON HENRIETTE MARIE (California, 1925)
**Charles Péguy et les Cahiers de la Quinzaine.*

†FICHTER, WILLIAM LEOPOLD (Columbia, 1926)
Lope de Vega's "El Castigo del Discreto". New
York. Instituto de las Españas, 1925. 283 p.
26-9038

†FIELD, HUGH FORSAITH (Chicago, 1925) *Finite
modal usage in Dante's Italian prose.*

FISCHER, WALTHER PAUL (Pennsylvania, 1912)
*The literary relations between La Fontaine
and the "Astrée" of Honoré d'Urfé...* Philadelphia, Pa., 1913. x, 103 p. [Univ. of Pa.
publs. Series in Romanic langs. and lits. no. 6.]
14-12481

†FISHER, JOHN ROBERTS (Columbia, 1916) [ed.]
*La vie de Saint Eustache, par Pierre de Beau-
vais; pub. for the first time from the manuscripts of London and Paris, with introduction, notes and index, by John Roberts Fisher...* Lancaster, Pa., Press of the New Era
printing company, 1917. iii, 69 [1] p. "Reprinted from the Romanic review, vol. viii.,
no. 1, January-March 1917." [A free render-
ing, in verse, of an earlier Latin version.]
18-20423

FISHER, LIZETTE ANDREWS (Columbia, 1916)
*The mystic vision in the Grail legend and in
the Divine Comedy...* New York, Columbia
Univ. press, 1917. x, 1l., 148 p. 1l. [Half-title:
Columbia Univ. stud. in Eng. and comp. lit.]
17-14984

†FITE, ALEXANDER GREEN (Wisconsin, 1922) *A
study of MS. 627 of the Berne Library on the
epic poem Godfroi de Bouillon.* [No Ms. Wis.]

†FITZ-GERALD, JOHN DRISCOLL (Columbia, 1905)
*The versification of the Cuaderna Via, as found
in Berceo's Vida de Santo Domingo de Silos,*
New York, The Columbia Univ. press. 1905.
8ᵛᵒ, xiii, 112 p. [Facsimiles.]

FLETCHER, ROBERT HUNTINGTON (Harvard, 1901) *The Arthurian material in the chronicles of Great Britain and France* Pub. revised and expanded. Boston, Ginn, 1906. 8°, x, 313 p. [Harvard stud. and notes in philol. and lit., 10.] [Dept. Eng. lit.] [Deceased.]

†FLOYD, JUANITA HELM (Columbia, 1921) *Women in the life of Honoré de Balzac.* [New York, 1921] viii, [2] xiii-xxxiv p., 1l., 5-320 p., 1l. [French Ed. *Les femmes dans la vie de Balzac.* Trad. et introd. de la Princesse Catherine Radziwill, avec 17 lettres inédites de Mme. Hanska et trois portraits hors texte. Paris, 1926. Librairie Plon, xviii, 315 p.] 21-8201

FONTAINE, JOSEPH AUGUSTE (Johns Hopkins, 1886) *On the history of the auxiliary verbs in the Romance languages.* [Stud. of the Univ. of Nebraska, vol. I, no. 1. 1888, 66 p.]

†FORD, HARRY EGERTON (Columbia, 1921) *Modern Provençal phonology and morphology, studied in the language of Frédéric Mistral...* New York, Col. Univ. press, 1921. vi, 93 p. [Half-title: Col. Univ. stud. in Romance philol. and lit.] 22-337.

†FORD, JEREMIAH DENIS MATTHIAS (Harvard, 1897) *The Old Spanish sibilants.* Pub. in Stud. and notes in philol. and lit., 1900. vii, p. 1-182.

FOSTER, ELIZABETH A. (Smith, 1919) *Le dernier séjour de J. J. Rousseau à Paris, 1770-1778.* Pub. in Smith College stud. in mod. langs., vol. ii, nos. 2-3. 184 p.

FRANÇOIS, VICTOR E. (New York, 1906) **Influence of Walter Scott on Alfred de Vigny.* 169 p.

†FREEMAN, STEPHEN ALBERT (Harvard, 1923) **The development of Victor Hugo's theory of the grotesque before the Préface de Cromwell.*

†FREIN, PIERRE JOSEPH (John Hopkins, 1899) *Phonology of the Patois of Pleigne, (canton de Berne).

FROST, FRANCIS LE JAU (Johns Hopkins, 1901) "The Art de contemplacio" of Ramon Lull. Pub. with introd. and study of the lang. of author. Baltimore, 1903. 50 p. 3-29045

FUNDENBURG, GEORGE BAER (Columbia, 1919) Feudal France in the French epic: a study of French institutions in history and poetry... Princeton, N. J. 1918. 4 p. l., 121 p. 20-5147

GADSBY, HERBERT H. (New York, 1892) *Analytical and critical comparison of the Phormio of Terence and Les Fourberies de Scapin of Molière. 125 p.

GAGER, DELAYE (Columbia, 1925) French comment on American education. New York, Columbia U. press, 1925. xiii, 150 p. 25-20091

†GALLAND, JOSEPH STANISLAW (Wisconsin, 1914) *The poetic history of the Bouillon family.

†GALPIN, STANLEY LEMAN (Yale, 1904) Cortois and vilain as conceived by the French and Provençal poets of the twelfth, thirteenth, and fourteenth centuries. Pub. as "Cortois and vilain: a study of the distinction made between them by the French and Provençal poets of the twelfth, thirteenth, and fourteenth centuries." New Haven, Conn., Ryder's printing house, 1905. 104 p. 5-24862

GARNAND, HARRY JENNINGS (Columbia, 1926) The influence of Walter Scott on the works of Balzac. New York, Institut des Études Françaises. 1926. 160 p. 26-14513

GARNER, SAMUEL (Johns Hopkins, 1881) The gerundial construction in the Romance languages. Baltimore, 1886-89. [Mod. lang. notes,

2:55-59, 136-141: 3: 93-96, 132-135, 213-219;
4: 67-73, 129-137.]

†GARVER, MILTON STAHL (Yale, 1904) *Sources of the allusions to animals in the Italian lyric of the thirteenth century.* Pub. as "Sources of the beast similes in the Italian lyric of the thirteenth century," in *Romanische Forschungen*, Erlangen, 1908. xxi, p. 276-320.

GEBERT, OTTO CARL (Stanford, 1920) *Les termes techniques militaires dans les traductions françaises de Végèce.* 241 p.

†GEDDES, JAMES, JR. (Harvard, 1894) *Study of an Acadian dialect. Revised, and pub. as "Study of an Acadian-French dialect spoken on the north shore of the Baie-des-Chaleurs".* Halle a.S., Niemeyer, 1908. xviii, 318, map. 9-16559

GEHLKE, CHARLES ELMER (Columbia, 1914) *Émile Durkheim's contributions to sociological theory...* New York, 1915. 2 p. l., 7-189 p. [Pub. also as Stud. in hist. econ. and pub. law, ed. by the Faculty of pol. science of Col. Univ. Vol. LXIII, no. 1; whole no. 151.] 15-5963

†GERIG, JOHN LAWRENCE (Nebraska, 1902) *Romance Semantics.*

†GILBERT, DONALD MONROE (Wisconsin, 1921) *The personal accusative in the works of Blasco Ibáñez.* 174 p.

GILL, JOHN GLANVILLE (Harvard, 1906) *Agglutination as a process of word formation in French.*

GILLESPY, FRANCES LYTLE (California, 1914) *Layamon's Brut; a comparative study in narrative art.* Univ. of California. Publs. in modern philol., vol. iii, no. 4, Berkeley, Cal., 1916. A16-1497

†GILMAN, MARGARET (Bryn Mawr, 1925) *Othello in French.* Paris, Édouard Champion, 1925. vii, [1] 197, [1] p., 1l. 25-24145

†GIRARD, WILLIAM (California, 1915) *Du transcendantalisme, considéré essentiellement dans sa définition et ses origines françaises.* Univ. of Calif. Publs. in mod. philol. vol. iv, no. 3, Berkeley, Cal., 1916. 17-1234

†GODDARD, EUNICE RATHBONE (Johns Hopkins, 1925) *Women's costume in French texts of the eleventh and twelfth centuries.* [Just pub.]

†GOGGIO, CHARLES (Wisconsin, 1920) **L'uso in Italiano del condizionale passato per il presente dello stesso modo.* 93 p.

†GOGGIO, EMILIO (Harvard, 1917) *Italian influences on Longfellow.* Part pub. as "The dawn of Italian culture in America," Romanic review, 1919. x: 250-262: "Italian influences on Longfellow's works," ibid., 1925. xvi: 208-222.

GOLDBERG, ISAAC (Harvard, 1912) *Don José Echegaray: a study in modern Spanish drama.* Pub. as "The drama of transition; native and exotic playcraft," Cincinnati, Stewart, Kidd Co., 1922. 487 p.

GORDON, ARTHUR (Cornell, 1909) **Spanish verse and versification in the 16th century.*

GOULD, WILLIAM ELFORD (Johns Hopkins, 1903) *The subjunctive mood in Don Quijote de la Mancha.* Baltimore, 1905. 35 p. 6-37895

†GRANT, ELLIOT MANSFIELD (Harvard, 1923) *The relations of poetry to industry under Louis Philippe and Napoleon III.* A part revised and pub. as "Poetry and modern industry: a literary controversy of the Second Empire", PMLA, 1924. xxxix: p. 932-962.

GREGORY, ALLENE (Radcliffe, 1913) *The French*

revolution and the English novel. . . New York
and London, G. P. Putnam's sons, 1915. xi,
337 p. 15-5033

†GRIMM, CHARLES (Yale, 1923) *Phonology, morphology, and glossary of the Libru di la Con-
questa di Sicilia per Manu di lu Conti Rugeri
di Normandia.* iv, 201, 8 p.

†GRUENBAUM, GUSTAV (Johns Hopkins, 1912)
*The Italian partitiv construction in the func-
tion of direct object.*

GRUNDLER, AUGUSTUS FERDINAND (Wisconsin,
1924) *Growth, in the "Miracles de Notrc
Dame"* [MS. Cange]. 110 p.

†GUYER, FOSTER ERWIN (Chicago, 1920) *The influence of Ovid on Crestien de Troyes.* [New
York, 1921] 2 p. l., p. 97-134, 216-247. ["Private edition, distributed by the Univ. of Chi.
libraries". "Reprinted from the Romanic review, vol. XII, nos. 2 and 3, April-June and
July-September, 1921".] 22-3980

†HACKER, EMIL FREDERIC (Wisconsin, 1921) *The
infinitive in French from 1300 to 1450.* 84 p.

†HAGBOLDT, PETER HERMAN (Chicago, 1924) *The
specific environment of romanticism.* [D. Ger.]

HAINES, GLADYS PRISCILLA (Yale, 1924) *Joseph
de Maistre; his works and his guiding princi-
ples.* v, 356 p.

HALL, HENRY MARION (Columbia, 1912) *Idylls
of fishermen; a history of the literary species.*
New York, 1912. xi, 217 p. [Columbia Univ.
stud. in comp. lit. no. 13.] [Contents: Origins
of the pastoral of fishers.—Sannazaro and his
imitators of the continent.—The English fisher idylls.—Appendix.—Bibliography (p. 201-
211). Chronological list of the chief English
piscatories.] 12-18273

†HALLEY, ALBERT ROBERTS (Harvard, 1923) *The Influence of Dante on the nineteenth century English poets. [Dept. Eng. lit.]

HAMILTON, ARTHUR (Johns Hopkins, 1914) *Sources of the religious element in Flaubert's Salammbô.* Baltimore, The Johns Hopkins press, 1918. i p. l., 32 p. 1l. ["An incomplete reprint from the Elliott monographs, no. 4. xi, 123 p."] [Also, Paris and Balto., 1917. xi, 123 p.] 18-23390 and 18-20222

†HAMILTON, GEORGE LIVINGSTONE (Columbia, 1903) *The indebtedness of Chaucer's Troilus and Criseyde to Guido delle Colonne's Historia trojana.* New York. The Col. Univ. press, 1903. 12mo., vi, 159 p. 3-2055

†HAMILTON, THEODORE ELY (Missouri, 1908) *The Cyclic relations of the Chanson de Willame.* Columbia, Mo., Univ. of Mo., 1911. ix, 301 p. [Publs. lit. and lang. Series. vol. II. Univ. of Mo. stud.] 11-28422

HANCOCK, ALBERT ELMER (Harvard, 1897) *Studies in the relations of the French Revolution and the English poets. With an appendix on some novels of the Revolution.* Pub., condensed and recast, as "The French Revolution and the English poets", New York, Holt, 1899. xvi, 197 p. [Dept. Eng. lit.] 99-797R

HANCOCK, JOHN LEONARD (Chicago, 1913) *Studies in stichomythia...* [Chicago, 1917] v, 97 p. ["A private edition distributed by the Univ. of Chicago libraries". "A trade edition is published by the Univ. of Chicago press, Chicago, Ill., 1917".] 17-15942

†HAPPEL, ALBERT PHILIP (Harvard, 1916) *The life and works of the Abbé de Saint-Réal.*

HARDY, CHARLES OSCAR (Chicago, 1916) *The negro question in the French revolution...*

Menasha, Wis., George Banta publishing company, 1919. 3 p. l., 91 p. 19-19277

†HARRY, PHILIP WARNER (Johns Hopkins, 1903) *A comparative study of the Aesopic fable in Nicole Bozon.* Cincinnati, 1905. 86 p. [Reprinted from Univ. of Cincinnati stud., 2nd series, vol. I., no. 2.] 5-36114

†HARVITT, HÉLÈNE JOSEPHINE (Columbia, 1913) *Eustorg de Beaulieu, a disciple of Marot, 1495(?)-1552...* Lancaster, Pa., Press of the New era printing co., 1918. ix, 164 p. ["Reprinted from the Romanic review, vol. v, no. 3 (1914), p. 252-275; vol. vi, no. 1 (1915), pp. 42-59; no. 2, pp. 206-218; no. 3, pp. 298-326; vol. vii, no. 1 (1916), pp. 83-109; vol. ix, no. 3 (1918) pp. 319-344.] 19-15144

†HASTINGS, WALTER SCOTT (Johns Hopkins, 1917) *The drama of Honoré de Balzac...* [Menasha, Wis., George Banta publishing company, 1920) 3 p. l., 158 p. 1l. 21-6697

†HATHEWAY, JOEL (Boston, 1926) *"Hubiera" and "Hubiese", from the period of the Cid to that of Cervantes, and including some of Spain's well-known XIXth century authors.* [In press.]

HAVENS, GEORGE REMINGTON (Johns Hopkins, 1917) *The abbé Prévost and English literature...* Baltimore, The Johns Hopkins press, 1921. 26 p. 1l. ["An incomplete reprint from the Elliott monographs, no. 9."] 21-17820

HAWKINS, RICHARD LAURIN (Harvard, 1908) *The life and works of Maistre Charles Fontaine, parisien.* In Harvard stud. in Romance langs., II, Cambridge, 1916. 8ᵛᵒ., vi, 288 p. [Condensed version of thesis.] 16-15611

†HAXO, HENRY EMIL (Chicago, 1913) *Denis Piramus: "La vie seint Edmunt"* (twelfth century)... Chicago, 1915. 57 p. [Reprinted

with additions from Modern philology, vol.
XII, nos. 6. and 9.] 15-16281·

†HEATON, HARRY CLIFTON (Columbia, 1916) [ed.]
...The Gloria d'amor of Fra Rocaberti; a Catalan vision-poem of the 15th century; ed. with
introd. notes, and glossary, by H. C. Heaton...
New York, Col. Univ. press, 1916. 4 p. l. [xii]-
ix p., 1l., 167 p., 1l. [Col. Univ. stud. in Romance philol. and lit.] 17-6377

HELLER, W. I. (New York, 1914) *Jean-Jacques
Rousseau and the origins of· French romanticism. 140 p.

†HENDRIX, WILLIAM SAMUEL (Chicago, 1923)
*Some native comic types in the early Span-
ish drama.

HENRÍQUEZ UREÑA, PEDRO (Minnesota, 1918)
La versificación irregular en la poesía caste-
llana. Madrid. [Revista de filología española.]
1920. 3 p. l., [V] VII, [I], 338 p. [Half-title:
Publicaciones de la "Revista de filología española". At head of title: Junta para amplia-
ción de estudios e investigaciones científicas,
Centro de estudios históricos.] 21-11254

HERRICK, LOUIS ROWELLE (Wisconsin, 1919)
*Contribution of the fabliaux to our knowledge
of mediaeval civilization. 138 p.

†HESPELT, E. HERMAN (Cornell, 1925 [Feb.])
*Fernán Caballero. A study of her life and
works.

†HILL, JOHN M. (Wisconsin, 1913) A contribution to Old Spanish lexicography... [In Univ.
of Wis. Abstracts of theses. Madison, 1917.
Vol. I, p. 109-136.] [Abstract of thesis.]
19-16893

†HILL, RAYMOND THOMPSON (Yale, 1911) La
Mule sanz Frain: an Arthurian romance by

Paiens de Maisières, ed. with introd., notes, and glossary. Baltimore, J. H. Furst co., 1911. 71 p.

†HILLS, ELIJAH CLARENCE (Colorado, 1906) *New Mexican Spanish.* PMLA., VOL. XXI.

†HOLBROOK, RICHARD THAYER (Columbia, 1902) *Dante and the animal kingdom.* New York, The Columbia Univ. press, 1902. 12ᵐᵒ., xviii, 376 p.

†HOLMES, HENRY ALFRED (Columbia, 1923) *Martín Fierro; an epic of the Argentine.* New York, Instituto de las Españas en los Estados Unidos, 1923. 2 p. l. 7-183 p. 23-7819

†HOLMES, URBAN TIGNER, JR. (Harvard, 1923) *The position of the unemphatic object pronoun in Old French.* A part of results pub. as "Die betonten, objektpronomina mit unpersönlichen verben," Zeitschr. f. Rom. philol., 1925. xliv: 337-339.

†HOLZKNECHT, KARL JULIUS (Pennsylvania, 1923) *Literary patronage in the middle ages.* Philadelphia, 1923. v p., 1l., 258 p. [Dep. of Eng. lit.] 24-5624

†HOPKINS, ANNETTE BROWN (Chicago, 1912)... *The influence of Wace on the Arthurian romances of Crestien de Troyes...* Menasha, Wis., George Banta publishing co., 1913. 4 p. l., 155 p. [Dept. of Eng. lit.] 13-24043

HORNICEK, JOHN (Harvard, 1922) **Madame Cottin: a study of the pre-romantic novel in France.*

†HOUSE, RALPH EMERSON (Chicago, 1909) *The "Comedia radiana" of Agustin Ortiz,* with introd. and notes. Chicago, 1910. 50 p.

†HOUSE, ROY TEMPLE (Chicago, 1917) [ed.]... *L'Ordene de Chevalerie; an old French poem,*

text, with introd. and notes... by Roy Temple House... Chicago, Ill., 1918. 2 p. l., 69 p. ["Private edition, distributed by the Univ. of Chicago libraries."] 19-9295 [Also, U. of Okla. Bulletin]

†HUBERT, MERTON JEROME (Cornell, 1924) *Novels and dramas of Paul Hervieu.*

HUDSON, MARGARET (Pennsylvania, 1927) *Juxtaposition of accents at the rime in French versification.* [U. of Pa. publs. Series in Rom. langs. and lits., no. 19.] [In press.]

†HUFFMAN, CHARLES HERBERT (Virginia, 1920) *The eighteenth-century novel in theory and practice.* Dayton, Va., The Ruebush Kieffer company [1923] 4 p. l., [7]-138 p. [Dept. of Eng. lit.] 23-14507

†HUTCHINGS, CHESLEY MARTIN (Harvard, 1922) *The sentiment of nationality in Spanish literary criticism from 1400 to 1621.*

HYMA, ALBERT (Michigan, 1922) *The "Devotio moderna" or Christian renaissance (1380-1520).* Grand Rapids, Mich., The Reformed press [1924]. xxxvi, 191. [The first 3 chapters of a work in 8 chapters, entitled "The Christian renaissance".] 24-20628

INGRAHAM, EDGAR SHUGART (Pennsylvania, 1903) *The sources of "Les Amours" of Jean Antoine de Baïf.* Columbus, 1905. 60. 5-30676

IVES, ANNETTE (Johns Hopkins, 1926) *La sensibilité esthétique d' Eugène Fromentin.*

†JACK, WILLIAM SHAFFER (Pennsylvania, 1923) *The early entremés in Spain: the rise of a dramatic form.* Philadelphia, 1923. 136 p. [On cover: Univ. of Pa. publs. Series in Romanic langs. and lits. no. 8] 23-17338

JAECK, EMMA GERTRUDE (Illinois, 1910) *Madame*

de Staël and the spread of German literature...
New York, Oxford Univ. press, Amer. branch,
1915. VI, 3-358 p. [Published also in German
lit. and culture; a series of monographs, ed.
by J. Goebel.] 15-15219

JAGEMANN, HANS CARL G. VON (Johns Hopkins,
1884) *Anglo-Norman vowel system in its relations to the Norman words in English.* 1884.
[Amer. philol. assoc. Trans., XV: 66-87] [De-
ceased, Jan. 21, 1926.]

†JENKINS, THOMAS ATKINSON (Johns Hopkins,
1894) *L'Espurgatoire Seint Patriz of Marie de
France; an Old-French poem of the Twelfth
Century.* Pub. with an introd. and a study of
the lang. of the author. Philadelphia, A. J.
Ferris, 1894. 149 p.

JODOCIUS, JEAN BAPTISTE ALBERT CAMILLE
(Pennsylvania, 1896) *Les allégories mytho-
logiques et les enseignements contenus dans
l'Ovide Moralisé.* 103 p.

†JOHNSON, OLIVER MARTIN (Johns Hopkins, 1896)
*The historical syntax of the atonic personal
pronouns in Italian.* Toronto, 1898. xii, 67 p.

†JONES, ANNE CUTTING (Bryn Mawr, 1926)
*Frederick Melchior Grimm, as a critic of
eighteenth century French Drama.* The Col-
legiate press, George Banta pub. co., Menasha,
Wis., 1926. 69 p.

JONES, FLORENCE NIGHTINGALE (Chicago, 1903)
The sources of Le Barbier de Séville. Chicago,
1908. 29 p.

†JONES, HARRIE STUART VEDDER (Harvard, 1906)
*Chaucer's Squire's Tale: an investigation of
the English fragment, the Old French "Cleomades", and analogous folk-tales.* Pub. in part,
in abbrev. form, as "Some observations upon
the Squire's Tale," in PMLA. 1905. XX: 346-

359; "The Cleomades [etc.]" in Journ. Eng.
and Germ. philol., 1906-07. VI: 221-243; and
"The Cleomades and related folk-tales, PMLA.
1908. XXIII: 557-598. [Dept. Eng. lit.]

JORDAN, BRADY RIMBEY (Wisconsin, 1926, Sum.
Sess.) *Influence of the Dreyfus affair upon
prominent literary figures.* 228 p.

KAHN, LINA (Columbia, 1916) *Metaphysics of
the supernatural as illustrated by Descartes...*
New York, Columbia Univ. press. 1918. viii,
65, [1] p., 1l. [Published also as Archives of
philosophy, no. 9.] 18-9795

†KANE, ELISHA KENT (Harvard, 1926) *Gongorism and the artistic culture of the Golden Age.*

KANY, CHARLES EMIL (Harvard, 1920) *The
beginning of the epistolary novel in Romance
languages.*

†KEIDEL, GEORGE CHARLES (Johns Hopkins, 1895)
ed. *Évangile aux femmes, an Old-French satire
on women.* Ed. with introd. and notes. Baltimore, 1895. 93 p. [Pub. also as Romance and
other stud. no. 1.]

KELLY, CALEB GUYER (Johns Hopkins, 1916)
French Protestantism, 1559-1562. Baltimore,
1918. viii, 9-186 p. [Pub. also as Johns Hopkins Univ. stud. in hist. and pol. science. Series
XXXVI, no. 4.] 19-98

†KENISTON, RALPH HAYWARD (Harvard, 1911)
*Garcilaso de la Vega: a critical edition of his
works, together with a life of the poet.* Enlarged and pub. as "Garcilaso de la Vega: a
critical study of his life and works". New
York, Hispanic Soc. of A., 1922. xii, 509 p.;
"Garcilaso de la Vega. Works; a critical text
with bibliog., ibid., xxiv, 453 p. 22-10021

KERR, WILLIAM ALEXANDER ROBB (Harvard,

1904) *Platonic love theories in the Renaissance, with special regard to France.* Results pub. in part as "Le cercle d'amour," in PMLA., 1904. XIX, p. 33-63; "Antoine Héroet's 'Parfaite Amye'," ibid., 1905. XX, 567-583; and "The Pléiade and Platonism," in Modern philology, 1908. V, p. 407-421.

KING, HELEN MAXWELL [Mrs. Helen King Gettiman] (Bryn Mawr, 1917) *Les doctrines littéraires de la Quotidienne, 1814-1830...* Durham, N. C. The Seeman printery, 1920. Cover-title, vii, 8-260, iv p., 11. [Reprinted from the Smith college stud. in modern lang. vol. I"] 21-13326.

KLEIN, JULIUS (Harvard, 1915) *The Mesta; a study in Spanish economic history, 1273-1836.* Cambridge, Harvard Univ. press, 1920. xviii, 444 p. 11. [Half-title: Harvard econ. stud. vol. XXI.] "Awarded the David A. Wells prize for the year 1917-1918, and pub. from the income of the David A. Wells fund." 21-694 [D. Hist.]

†KNICKERBOCKER, WILLIAM EDWIN (Columbia, 1911) *Ellipsis in Old French.* New York, 1911. 12mo, 155 p. A11-1071

KRAPPE, ALEXANDER HAGGERTY (Chicago, 1919) *... Alliteration in the Chanson de Roland and in the Carmen de prodicione Guenonis...* Iowa City, Ia. [The Athens print shop] 1921. 3 p. l., 82 p. 21-7216

KUERSTEINER, ALBERT FREDERICK (Johns Hopkins, 1904) *The use of the relative pronoun in the Rimado de Palacio.* Paris, 1911. 125 p. [Reprinted from the Revue hispanique, vol. xxiv: 46-170.] [Deceased.] 13-14242

†KURZ, HARRY (Columbia, 1916) *European characters in French drama of the eighteenth century...* New York, Col. Univ. press. 1916. xii,

329 [1] p. [Col. Univ. stud. in Romance philol. and lit.] 16-11196

LACOMBE, LEO GEORGE (Stanford, 1922) *The place of modernism in French thought, with special reference to Alfred Loisy. 108 p.

LAIGLE, MATHILDE (Columbia, 1912) Le Livre des Trois Vertus de Christine de Pisan, et son milieu historique et littéraire. Avec deux planches hors texte. Pub. in the Bibliothèque du XVe Siècle, vol. XVI, Paris, H. Champion, 1912. xii, 375 p. 13-15911

LAMB, WILLIAM WHITFIELD (New York, 1911) The syntax of the Heptameron... New York, 1914. iv, 178 p. 15-4465

LAMOURET, GEORGES (New York, 1911) *Le théâtre français au XVIIIe siècle. 136 p.

†LANCASTER, HENRY CARRINGTON (Johns Hopkins, 1907) The French tragi-comedy, its origin and development from 1552-1628. Baltimore, 1907. xxvi, 189 p. 7-23332

LANDES, MARGARET WINIFRED (Yale, 1923) A suggested interpretation of Bergson's doctrine of intuition. [Boston, 1924] cover-title, [1], [450], 462 p. ["Reprinted from the Philosophical rev. vol. XXXIII, no. 5, Sept. 1924"] 24-31612

LANGER, HELEN MARY (Wisconsin, 1921) *The doctor in the French drama. 125 p.

†LANGLEY, ERNEST FELIX (Harvard, 1909) The poetry of Giacomo da Lentino (Sicilian school); critical edition, in Harvard stud. in Romance langs. I, Cambridge, 1915. 8vo, XLI, 150 p.

†LANSING, RUTH (Radcliffe, 1914) *Treatment of woman in Spanish literature of the thirteenth, fourteenth and fifteenth centuries.

LAUBSCHER, GUSTAV GEORGE (Johns Hopkins,

1909) *The past tenses in French. A study of certain phases of their meaning and function.* Baltimore, 1909. 60 p. [Deceased, 1918.]

†LEAVITT, STURGIS ELLENO (Harvard, 1917) *Scarron in England, 1656-1800.* Part modified and pub. as "Paul Scarron and English travesty," Harv. stud. in philol., 1919. XIV: 108-120.

†LEBERT, EUGENE MARIE (Wisconsin, 1924) **L'imagination d'Alfred de Vigny et la science de son époque et autres additions à sa biographie intellectuelle.* [Ed. R.M.M. No MS. Wis. lib.]

†LE DUC, ALMA DE LANDE (Columbia, 1916) *Gontier Col and the French pre-renaissance...* New York, 1918. vii, 103, [1] p. [Reprinted from the Romanic rev. vol. vii, no. 4, 414-457, 1916; vol. viii, no. 2, 145-165, and no. 3, 290-306, 1917.] 19-9562

LEFTWITCH, FLORENCE [Mrs. S. Priolean Ravenel] (Bryn Mawr, 1906) *"La Vie Saint Edmund le Rei". An Anglo-Norman poem of the twelfth century by Denis Piramus.* Philadelphia, The John C. Winston Co., 1906. 8ᵛᵒ., l, x, 174 p. [Reprint from the Bryn Mawr College monograph series, vol. V.]

†LEVENGOOD, SIDNEY LAWRENCE (Princeton, 1925) *The use of colour in the verse of the Pléiade.* [In press.]

LEVINE, LOUIS (Columbia, 1912) *The labor movement in France; a study in revolutionary syndicalism.* New York, 1912. 1 p. l., 5-213 p. [Pub. also as Stud. in hist., econ., and pub. law, ed. by the Faculty of pol. science of Col. Univ., vol. XLVI, no. 3, whole no. 116.] 12-18305

†LEVY, RAPHAEL (Johns Hopkins, 1924) **A contribution to Old French lexicography based on*

*Hagen's translation of the astrological works
of Abraham Ibn Ezra.*

LEWIS, EDWIN SEELYE (Johns Hopkins, 1892)
Guernsey: its people and dialect. Baltimore,
1895. 82 p. [Reprinted from the PMLA., Vol.
X, no. 1.] 15-9378

LHEVINNE, ISADORE (Pennsylvania, 1924) *The
language of the Glossary Sangallensis 912 and
its relationship to the language of other Latin
glossaries.* [U. of Pa. Series in Rom. langs.
and lits., no. 14, 1924. 78 p.] 26-13564

LINTON, ANNE (Pennsylvania, 1921)

LINTON, ELISABETH   ”   ”   *Pascal's
mystic hexogram; its history and graphical
representation, by Anne and Elisabeth Linton...* Philadelphia, Pa., 1921. 17 p., 14, l.
[Ed. R. M. M. The authors' thesis; done in
collaboration; Anne and Elisabeth Linton; a
double Ph. D.] 21-18664

†LISTER, JOHN THOMAS (Chicago, 1920) [ed.]
*...Perlesvaus, Hatton Manuscript 82, branch
1...* Menasha, Wis., George Banta publishing
company, 1921. 3 p. l., 87 p. 21-14285

†LITTLE, ROBERT IRVING (Harvard, 1918) **The
moral ideas of Chrétien de Troyes.*

LIVINGSTON, ALBERT ARTHUR (Columbia, 1911)
*I sonetti morali ed amorosi di Gian Francesco
Busenello (1598-1659.) Testo critico.* Venice,
G. Fabbris, 1911. 8ᵛᵒ., 144 p.

†LIVINGSTON, CHARLES HAROLD (Harvard, 1920)
*The Latin Prefix "ex" in French.

LODEMAN, FRANK EMIL (Cornell, 1895) *La Pas
Saladin; an old French poem of the Third
Crusade,* Baltimore, 1897. 27 p. [Deceased,
1908.]

LOGIE, THOMAS (Johns Hopkins, 1890) *Phonology of the Patois of Cachy (Somme.)* Baltimore, 1892. 73 p. [Reprinted from the PMLA., vol. vii, no. 4.] 3-29682

LONG, WILLIAM JOHN (Pennsylvania, 1909) *The dramas of Philippe Quinault.* [No MS. Pa.]

LORENZ, THEODORE CHARLES GUILLAUME (Pennsylvania, 1897) *Molière et ses emprunts; aperçu général.* 153 p. [Deceased.]

†LOWE, LAWRENCE FRANCIS HAWKINS (Princeton, 1923) *Gérard de Nevers, a study of the prose version of the Roman de la violette.* Princeton. [Mâcon, Protat frères, imprimeurs] 1923. 4 p. l., 72 p. 1l. [Issued also as Elliott monographs in the Romance langs. and lits. no. 13.] 24-4143

†LUKER, BENJAMIN FRANKLIN (Columbia, 1916) *The use of the infinitive instead of a finite verb in French...* New York, Columbia Univ. press, 1916. 5 p. l., 113, [1] p. 1l. [Col. Univ. stud. in Romance philol. and lit.] 16-23611

†LUQUIENS, FREDERICH BLISS (Yale, 1905) *The Roman de la Rose and medieval Castilian literature.* Pub. in the *Romanische Forschungen,* Erlangen, 1907. XX, p. 284-320.

McCABE, THOMAS (Johns Hopkins, 1888) *The morphology in Francesco Petrarca's Canzoniere, accompanied by a general introduction and a critical glossary.* [Deceased, 1891.]

†MACCLINTOCK, LANDER (Chicago, 1917) *Saint-Beuve's critical theory and practice after 1849...* Chicago, Ill., The University of Chicago press, 1920. 1 p. l., v-ix, 161 p. 20-16366.

MACKENZIE, DONALD ALEXANDER (Pennsylvania, 1910) [ed.]... *Diálogo de la vida de los pajes* de palacio, compuesto por Diego de Hermosilla... ed. with an introd. and notes by Donald Mackenzie... Valladolid, [España], Imp. y lib. Viuda de Montero, 1916. 255 p. [Publs. of the Univ. of Pa. Series in Romanic langs. and lits. no. 7.] 21-21589

†McKENZIE, KENNETH (Harvard, 1895) *The development of Italian lyric poetry before the rise of the "dolce stil nuovo".* Revised in part, and pub. as "A sonnet ascribed to Chiaro Davanzati and its place in fable literature" in PMLA., 1898. XIII, p. 205-220.

†McKIBBEN, GEORGE FITCH (Chicago, 1905) *"The Eructavit", an old French poem; the author's environment, his argument and materials,* Baltimore, 1907. 45 p. 7-41443

†McLEOD, MALCOLM (Harvard, 1914) *French influence on English drama during the first forty years of the nineteenth century* [Dept. Eng. lit.]

McMAHON, AMOS PHILIP (Harvard, 1916) *The mediaeval conception of tragedy and comedy. Part pub. as "On the second book of Aristotle's Poetics and the source of Theophrastus's definition of tragedy,"* Harv. stud. class. philol., 1917. xxviii: p. 1-46. [Dept. compar. lit.] 18-10199

McMAHON, *Sister* MARY CATHARINE [Of The Ursuline Nuns, Cleveland, Ohio] (Catholic Sisters' College, Brookland, D. C., 1925) *Aesthetics and Art in the Astrée of Honoré d'Urfé.* Printed at Washington, D. C. 1925. 26-16190

McMURPHY, SUSANNAH JANE (U. of Washington, 1923) *Spenser's use of Ariosto for allegory.* Seattle, Univ. of Wash. press [1924] 54 p. [Univ. of Wash. publs. lang. and lit. V. 2. Feb. 1924.] 25-10531

Mc PIKE, ELIZABETH (Chicago, 1923) *Aristotelian and pseudo-Aristotelian elements in Corneille's tragedies.

†MALAKIS, EMILE (Pennsylvania, 1925) French travellers in Greece (1770-1820), an early phase of French Philhellenism. [U. of Pa. Series in Romanic langs. and lits., no. 15, 1925. 90 p.] 26-7186

MALLARIAN, CASBAR HAGOP (Cornell, 1898) *The dramatic treatment of the human actions and passions in the tragedies and comedies of Corneille. [Deceased, 1904.]

†MANN, ALBERT, JR. (Harvard, 1923) *Spanish satiric verse from the earliest times to the end of the sixteenth century.

†MANTZ, HAROLD ELMER (Columbia, 1917) French criticism of American literature before 1850... New York, Col. Univ. press, 1917. viii p. 1l., 165, [1] p. [Half-title: Col. Univ. stud. in Romance philol. and lit.] 17-15471

†MARDEN, CHARLES CARROLL (Johns Hopkins, 1894) The phonology of the Spanish dialect of Mexico City. Baltimore, 1896. 66 p. [Reprinted from the PMLA, vol. iv. no. 1.] 3-22020

MARTELL, DANIEL ERNEST (Pennsylvania, 1902) The dramas of Don Antonio de Solís y Rivadeneyra. Phila., 1902. 57 p. 3-26500

†MASON, JAMES FREDERICK (Johns Hopkins, 1911) The melodrama in France from the revolution to the beginning of romantic drama, 1791-1830. Chapter I... Baltimore, J. H. Furst company, 1912. 3 p. l., ix-xv, 39 p. 13-4093

MATTHEWS, CHARLES EUGLEY (Johns Hopkins, 1908) Cist and cil; a syntactical study. Baltimore, 1907. x, 117 p.

MATZKE, JOHN ERNST (Johns Hopkins, 1888)

*Dialektische eigentümlichkeiten in der ent-
wickelung des mouillierten l im altfranzösi-
schen.* Baltimore, 1888. 56 p. [Reprinted from
the PMLA., Vol. V. no. 2.] [Deceased, 1910.]

MENGER, LOUIS EMIL (Johns Hopkins, 1893)
*The historical development of the possessive
pronouns in Italian.* Baltimore, 1893. VI, 69 p.
[Reprinted from the PMLA., New Series. I,
No. 2.] [Deceased, 1903.] 11-2463

†MENUT, ALBERT DOUGLAS (Columbia, 1922) *The
semantics of doublets studied in Old and Middle French.* New York, 1922. 2 p. l., 7-175 p.
[The study is restricted to words appearing
textually in the period preceding 1530. cf.
Pref.] 23-1554

MÉRAS, ALBERT A. (New York, 1908) *The Genesis of the Monroe Doctrine.* [Deceased, 1926.]

†MEREDITH, JOSEPH ARTHUR (Pennsylvania,
1925) *"Introits" and "Loa" in the Spanish
drama of the sixteenth century.* Phila. [U. of
Pa. Series in Rom. langs. and lit. no. 16.]

†MERRILL, ROBERT VALENTINE (Chicago, 1923)
The Platonism of Joachim du Bellay. Chicago,
Chicago Univ. press, 1925.

MICHELL, ROBERT BELL (Wisconsin, 1911) *The
poetic history of Duc Naime of Bavière.*

†MILLER, JOHN RICHARDSON (Harvard, 1922)
*The reputation of Boileau in France in the
eighteenth century.*

†MILLER, META HELENA (Johns Hopkins, 1922)
Chateaubriand and English Literature. Balto.
J. H. U. press, 1925. 204 p. [J. H. U. stud. R.
lit. iv.]

MILLER, PAUL GERARD (Wisconsin, 1914) *The
Spanish version of the Poem of Alexander.*

MITCHELL, JULIA POST (Columbia, 1916) *St. Jean de Crèvecoeur*... New York, Columbia Univ. press, 1916. xvi, 1l., 362 p. [Columbia Univ. stud. in Eng. and comp. lit.] ["Reprints from Crèvecoeur", p. 346-350.] 17-6368

MOLENAER, SAMUEL PAUL (Columbia, 1899) *Li Livres du Gouvernement des Rois, a thirteenth century French version of Egidio Colonna's treatise, "De Regimine Principium"*. Now first pub. from the Kerr MS. together with introd. and notes and full-page facsimile. New York. The Macmillan Co., 1899. 8ᵛᵒ., xlii, 161 p. [Deceased.]

†MOORE, CLARENCE KING (Harvard, 1906) *An historical study of the Spanish preposition "a" with the accusative case.*

†MOORE, OLIN HARRIS (Harvard, 1913) *The Young King: Henry Plantagenet (1155-1183) in literature and tradition.* Portions pub. in the Romanic review, 1913. IV, p. 1-26; 1914. V, p. 45-54; in Romania, 1925. Li: 46-75. Ohio State Univ. stud., 1925. no. xii, 2: viii, 107 [Contrib. in lang. and lit., 3.]

†MORLEY, SYLVANUS GRISWOLD (Harvard, 1902) *Spanish influence on Molière.* Portions pub. in PMLA., 1904. XIX, p. 270-290.

MORRISON, ALFRED JAMES (Johns Hopkins, 1903) *Character-study in Old French romans d'aventure: The heroine.* [Deceased, 1923.]

†MOSELEY, THOMAS ADDIS EMMET (Johns Hopkins, 1915) *The "lady" in comparisons from the poetry of the "dolce stil nuovo"*... Menasha, Wis., George Banta publishing company, 1916. 3 p. l., 65 p. 16-22708

†MOTT, LEWIS FREEMAN (Columbia, 1896) *The system of courtly love, studied as an introduc-*

tion to the Vita Nuova of Dante. Boston, Ginn and co., 1896. 8ᵛᵒ., vi, 156 p. A11-239

†MULLER, HENRI FRANÇOIS (Columbia, 1912) *Origine et histoire de la préposition "à" dans les locations du type de "faire faire quelque chose à quelqu'un".*.. Poitiers, Impr. A. Masson, 1912. 3 p. l., 199 p., 1l. 12-31062

†MURRAY, CHESTER (Cornell, 1908) *History of the speculations with regard to the personality of Dante's Beatrice from XIVth cent. down to the present time.*

†MYRICH, ARTHUR BECKMITH (Harvard, 1904) *Some notes on Italian borrowings from England in the eighteenth century.* [Dept. compar. lit.]

†NAYLOR, LOUIS HASTINGS (Johns Hopkins, 1923) *Chateaubriand and Virgil.*

NEFF, THEODORE LEE (Chicago, 1896) *La satire des femmes dans la poésie lyrique française du moyen âge.* Paris, 1900. x, 118 p. 4-9736

†NEUENSCHWANDER, ELISE (Yale, 1913) *Influence of Villon on Voltaire.*

†NICOLAY, ANNA SOPHIA CLARA LEONORA (Pennsylvania, 1907) *The life and works of Cristóbal de Castillejo, the last of the Nationalists in Castilian poetry.* [U. of P. publs. Series in Rom. langs. and lits., no. 4, 1910. 126 p.]

†NITZE, WILLIAM ALBERT (Johns Hopkins, 1899) *The Old-French Grail Romance Perlesvaus. A study of its principal sources.* Baltimore, 1902. 113 p. 3-26504 *Cancel

NOBLE, MARY ANNGENETTE (Yale, 1926) *The life and writings of Ernest Aimé Feydeau,* V, 350 p.

†NORMAN, HILDA LAURA (Chicago, 1924) *Indus-

*try and financial speculation in French drama
from 1800 to 1870.*

†NORTHUP, GEORGE TYLER (Chicago, 1906) *"El
libro de los gatos"; a text with introd. and
notes.* Chicago, 1908. 78 p.

†NYKL, A. R. (Chicago, 1921) **Rrekotamients del
Rrey Alisandere, an aljamiado text, with introd. and notes.*

O'CONNOR, BERNARD FRANCIS (Johns Hopkins,
1883) **The syntax of Villehardouin.* [De-
ceased, 1922.]

†OGDEN, PHILIP (Johns Hopkins, 1897) *A comparative study of the poem Guillaume d'Angleterre with a dialectic treatment of the manuscripts.* Baltimore, 1900. vii, 33 p. 1-5596

†OLMSTED, EVERETT WARD (Cornell, 1897) *The
sonnet in French literature and the development of the French sonnet form.* Ithaca, N.
Y. 1897. 214 p.

OSTRANDER, FREDERIC CURRY (Columbia, 1915)
[ed.]... *Li romans dou lis,* by F. C. Ostrander... New York, Columbia Univ. press. 1915.
v, 154 p. 1l. [Columbia Univ. stud. in Romance
philol. and lit.] [Deceased.] 16-6702

†PARKER, CLIFFORD STETSON (Columbia, 1925)
The defense of the Child by French novelists.
Menasha, Wis., C. S. Parker, in care of George
Banta pub. co., 1925. xi, 141 p. 25-10399

†PARKER, EUGENE FRED (Harvard, 1920) *Michel
Nostradamus, prophet.* Revised and trans. into French, and pub. as "La légende de Nostradamus et sa vie réelle". Rev. du XVIᵉ Siècle,
1923. X: 93-106, 148-158.

†PARMENTER, CLARENCE EDWARD (Chicago, 1922)
**The French Epistle in Verse from Deschamps
to the year 1549.*

†PATCH, HELEN ELIZABETH (Bryn Mawr, 1921) *The dramatic criticism of Théophile Gautier.* Bryn Mawr. Pa., 1922. viii, 165 p. ["Index alphabétique des auteurs dramatiques critiqués par Théophile Gautier (1835-1872)": p. 98-164.] 23-232

†PATRICK, GEORGE ZINOVEI (California, 1923) *Étude morphologique et syntaxique des verbes dans Maistre Pierre Pathelin.* [Berkeley, Calif., Univ. of Calif. press, 1924] 1 p. l., p. [287]-379. [Univ. of Calif. publs. in mod. philol. V. 8, no. 4.] 25-1248

†PATTERSON, SHIRLEY GALE (Cornell, 1911) *The Puy; a study of a pre-Renaissance literary influence in the north of France.*

PATZER, OTTO (Wisconsin, 1907) *Eustache Deschamps as a commentator upon the events and conditions of his time...* [In Univ. of Wis. Abstracts of theses. Madison, 1917. vol. i, p. (151)-168.] [Abstract of thesis.] 19-16895

PECKHAM, GEORGE WILLIAMS (Columbia, 1916) *Logic of Bergson's philosophy...* New York, [University printing office, Col. Univ.] 1917. vii, 68 p., 1l. [Pub. also as Archives of philos. no. 8.] 18-11439

PEIRCE, WALTER THOMSON (Johns Hopkins, 1906) *The bourgeois from Molière to Beaumarchais. The study of a dramatic type.* Columbus, F. J. Heer, 1907. 88 p. 7-24250

PELLISSIER, ROBERT ÉDOUARD (Harvard, 1913) *The neo-classic movement in Spain during the eighteenth century.* [Deceased, 1916]

PEOPLES, MARGARET (Smith, 1927-8) *La querelle Rousseau-Hume d'après les derniers documents.* [In process of revision.]

†PFLUEGER, LUTHER APPEL (Wisconsin, 1924)

*Voltaire's relations to English literature. 206 p.

†PHELPS, RUTH SHEPARD (Chicago, 1924) *An earlier form of Petrarch's Canzoniere.

PHILLIPS, ROY CLEVELAND (Wisconsin, 1924) *Crit. ed. of "La Francesilla", a drama by Lope de Vega. 339 p.

PHIPPS, HELEN (Columbia, 1925) Some aspects of the agrarian question in Mexico. Austin, U. of Texas, 1925. 157 p. 25-15619

PIERSON, ORIANA PAULINE (Illinois, 1926) *The Dramatic Works of Alain-René Lesage; an analytical and comparative study.

PIRAZZINI, AGIDE (Columbia, 1917) The influence of Italy on the literary career of Alphonse de Lamartine. New York, Columbia Univ. press, 1917. xii, 160 p. 1l. [Half-title: Columbia Univ. stud. in Romance philol. and lit.] 18-8104

†PLACE, EDWIN BRAY (Harvard, 1919) A study of the works of Salas Barbadillo and María de Zayas. Part pub. as "María de Zayas, an outstanding woman short story writer of seventeenth-century Spain". Univ. of Colo. stud., 1923. xiii: 1-56 p.

PORTER, MRS. ALICE DOWNEY (Cornell, 1899) *Religious drama in England and France from the beginning of the 9th to the close of the 13th century.

POST, CHANDLER RATHFON (Harvard, 1909) Castilian allegory of the fifteenth century, with especial reference to the influence of Dante. Pub. as "Mediaeval Spanish allegory" in Harvard stud. in comp. lit., IV, Cambridge, 1915. xii, 331 p. 15-8079

POTTER, MURRAY ANTHONY (Harvard, 1899)

[Assist. Prof. Romance Langs., Harvard Univ., 1907-1915.] *The epic theme of a combat between father and son; a study of its genesis and use in literature and popular tradition.* Pub. as "Sohrab and Rustum: the epic theme", etc. in the Grimm library, XIV, London, 1902. 8ᵛᵒ., xii, 234 p. [Deceased, 1915.]   3-543

DE POYEN-BELLISLE, RENÉ (Chicago, 1894) *Les sons et les formes du Créole dans les Antilles.* Baltimore, 1894. 62 p. [Deceased.]   19-2096

†PRESTON, ETHEL (Chicago, 1918) **Reappearing characters in Balzac.* III, 192 p. [10 pages of abstract.]

†PRICE, WILLIAM RALEIGH (Columbia, 1911) *The symbolism of Voltaire's novels, with special reference to Zadig.* New York, The Columbia Univ. press, 1911. 12ᵐᵒ., vi, 269 p. A11-2437

PRIESTLEY, HERBERT INGRAM (California, 1917) *José de Gálvez, visitor-general of New Spain, 1765-1771...* [Berkeley, 1916] cover-title, xiv, 449 p. [Univ. of Calif. publs. in hist., vol. v.] 17-18481

†PUGH, ANNE REESE (Columbia, 1923) *Michelet and his ideas on social reform.* New York. Col. Univ. press, 1923. xxxiv, 243 p. 1l. [Half-title: Col. Univ. stud. in Romance philol. and lit.] 23-13178

RAGGIO, ANDREW PAUL (Harvard, 1904) **A treatment of the development from popular Latin to Spanish of certain consonant groups ending in y.* [Deceased, 1917]

REDFIELD, JOHN HOWARD (Harvard, 1914) **The earlier Latin-Romance loan words in Basque and their bearing on the history of Basque and the neighboring Romance languages.*

†REED, FRANK OTIS (Harvard, 1905) **The his-*

tory of the Spanish past participle compounded with "haber".

REIFF, PAUL FRIEDRICH (Illinois, 1912) *Friedrich Gentz, an opponent of the French revolution and Napoleon...* Champaign-Urbana, Flanigan-Pearson Co., 1912. 159 p. [Pub. also as Univ. of Illinois stud. in the soc. sciences, vol. I, no. 4.] 13-3679

†REINHARD, JOHN REVELL (Harvard, 1921) *Amadas et Ydoine: a study in comparative literature.* Part pub. as "Amadas et Ydoine, roman du XIII⁰ siècle", Paris, Champion, 1926. x, 299 p. [Les Classiques Français du Moyen-Age.] [Also, "The Old French Romance of Amadas et Ydoine, an historical study." Revised. Durham, N. C., Duke Univ. press, 1927. VIII chapters, 220 p.] [For original material of Chaps. III, IV, V; see Romanic review, XV, (1924). 179-214, 215-265 pp.] [Dept. compar. lit.]

†RHODES, SOLOMON ALDHADEF (Cornell, 1925) *A Critical study of Baudelaire.*

RICE, CARL COSMO (Harvard, 1902) *The phonology of Gallic clerical Latin after the sixth century: an introductory historical study based chiefly on Merovingian and Carolingian spelling and on the forms of Old French loanwords.* Pub. by the author, Moscow, Idaho, 1909. 8ᵛᵒ., 120 p. [Abstract pub. in Proceeds Amer. Philol. Assoc., 1904. XXXV, p. LXIV, LXV.]

†RICE, JOHN PIERREPONT (Yale, 1909) *A critical edition of the Bestiary and Lapidary from the Acerba of Cecco d'Ascoli.*

†RICHARDSON, HENRY BRUSH (Yale, 1923) *A vocabulary to the Libro de Buen Amor of Juan Ruiz, Arcipreste de Hita.* IV, 193 p.

†RIDDELL, AGNES RUTHERFORD (Chicago, 1916) *Flaubert and Maupassant: a literary relationship...* Chicago, Ill., The Univ. of Chicago press [1920] 1 p. l., v-x, 120 p. 20-5184

†RIDDLE, LAWRENCE MELVILLE (Johns Hopkins, 1922) *The genesis and sources of Pierre Corneille's tragedies from Médée to Pertharite.* Baltimore. The Johns Hopkins press, 1926. 22 p. [The John Hopkins stud. in Romance lits. et langs. Vol. III.]

†ROBBINS, HARRY WOLCOTT (Minnesota, 1923) *Saint Edmund's "Merure de Seinte église", an early example of rhythmical prose.* Lewisburg, Pa. Univ. Print shop [1924] XLVII, 78., 1l. 25-464

†ROCKWOOD, ROBERT EVERETT (Harvard, 1924) **Don Juan Manuel, his conception and consideration of women.*

ROGERS, CORNELIA HEPHZIBAH BULKLEY (Yale, 1894) [Instructor, French & Italian, Vassar until 1903.] **Sinalefa, sinéresis é hiato en los romances del Cid.* [Deceased, 1903.]

ROLBIECKI, JOHN JOSEPH (Catholic U. of America, 1922) *The political philosophy of Dante Alighieri...* Washington, D. C., Catholic Univ. of America. 1921. 2 p. l., 7-157 p. 22-7760

†VAN ROOSBROECK, GUSTAVE L. (Minnesota, 1919) *A study of Corneille's evolution and personality.* Pub. in parts as follows: Corneille's early Friends and Surroundings. Mod. phil., Nov., 1920. The Cid Theme in France in 1600, Minneapolis, Pioneer press, 1920. The Source of Sallebray's "Amante Ennemie", Mod. lang. notes, Feb., 1921. The Purpose of Corneille's Cid, Minneapolis, 1921. The Genesis of Corneille's Mélite, Vinton, Iowa, 1921. Corneille's Relations with Louis Petit, Mod. lang. notes,

May, 1922. Corneille's Cinna and the Conspiration des Dames, Mod. phil., Aug., 1922. Un Document inconnu sur la Querelle du Cid; L'Anatomie du Cid, R. H. L., June, 1925. Chapelain décoiffé: A Battle of Parodies, PMLA, Dec., 1924. Preciosity in Corneille's early Plays, Phil. quart., Jan., 1927. The Dédicace of Corneille's Théodore. An early commentary on Corneille's Cid, Leuvensche, Bijdragen, June, 1925. Corneille's early Theories, Neo-Philologus, 1926. 166-172 p. [Ed. R. M. M. Other parts and translations to appear shortly.]

†Rose, Robert Selden (California, 1915) *Quevedo and El Buscón.

†Rosenberg, S. L. Millard (Pennsylvania, 1909) A critical edition of La Española de Florencia (O Burlas Veras, y Amor Invencionero) Comedia Famosa de Calderón de la Barca. [U. of Pa. publs. Series in Romanic langs. et lits., No. 5, 1911. 132 p.]

Ross, Leslie Truesdale (Wisconsin, 1921) *A general treatment of Rostand the dramatist.

Rougier, Francis L. (New York, 1911) *Plautus, his influence on French comedy. 166 p.

Roumiguière, Henriette (California, 1925) Le Français dans les relations diplomatiques: [U. of Calif. publs. in mod. philol., xii, 4.]

†Rudwin, Maximilian Josef (Columbia, 1922) Supernaturalism and satanism in Chateaubriand. Chicago [etc.] The Open court publishing company, 1922. 3 p. l., 50 p. ["This study... is to form the opening chapter of a book, which is to appear under the title, The devil in modern French literature." Pref. note.] ["Reprinted from the Open court, vol. XXXVI".] 23-1555

RUSSELL, FRANCES BAKER (Radcliffe, 1924) *The aesthetic idealism of Leconte de Lisle.*

†RUSSO, JOSEPH LOUIS (Columbia, 1922) *Lorenzo Da Ponte, poet and adventurer.* New York, Columbia Univ. press, 1922. xviii, 166 p., 1l. 22-17048

RUUTZ-REES, CAROLINE (Columbia, 1910) *Charles de Sainte-Marthe.* New York, The Columbia Univ. press, 1910. 12mo., xvi, 664 p. Trans. into French by Marcel Bonnet as Charles de Sainte-Marthe (1512-1555) Etude sur les premières années de la Renaissance Française. Préface de Abel Lefranc, professeur au College de France. Paris. Edouard Champion, 1919. 8vo., xxv, 387 p. [Couronné de l'Académie Française.] A11-2423

SAIT, MRS. UNA MIRRIELEES [née Bernard] (Columbia, 1914) *The ethical implications of Bergson's philosophy...* [New York] 1914. 183 p. [Pub. also as Archives of philos. no. 4 and Col. Univ. contrib. to philos. and psychol., vol. xviii, no. 3-4.] 14-16786

†SALVIO, ALFONSO DE (Harvard, 1904) *The verse endings and the rhyme in the Divina Commedia.*

SBEDICO, ATTILIO FILIPPO (Pennsylvania, 1909) *Giosuè Carducci.* [Deceased.] [No MS. U. Pa.]

SCHEIFLEY, WILLIAM H. (Pennsylvania, 1914) *...Brieux and contemporary French society...* [New York] The Knickerbocker press, G. P. Putnam's sons, 1917. x p., 1l., 436 p. 18-20430

†SCHENCK, EUNICE MORGAN (Bryn Mawr, 1914) *La part de Charles Nodier dans la formation des idées romantiques de Victor Hugo jusqu'à la préface de Cromwell...* Bryn Mawr,

Pa., 1914. x p., 1l., 149 p. [Pub. also as Bryn Mawr College monographs, monograph series, vol. 16.] 14-20276

†SCHLATTER, EDWARD BUNKER (Wisconsin, 1909) *The development of the vowel of the unaccented initial syllable in Italian...* [Madison, 1913] cover-title, 69 p. ["Reprinted June, 1913, from the Transactions of the Wis. academy of sciences, arts, and letters, vol. xvii, part II".] 15-8703

†SCHOENBERGER, HAROLD WILLIAM (Pennsylvania, 1924) *American adaptations of French plays on the New York and Philadelphia stages from 1790 to 1833.* Philadelphia, 1924. 99p. 24-25332

SCHUTZ, ALEXANDER HERMAN (Chicago, 1922) **Peasant vocabulary in the Works of George Sand.*

†SCHWARTZ, WILLIAM LEONARD (Stanford, 1926) **The imaginative interpretation of the Far East in post-Classical French literature.* 361 p.

†SCHWARZ, H. STANLEY (New York, 1923) **The relationship between the ideas in the prefaces and in the plays of Alexandre Dumas fils.* vi., 220 p.

†SEGALL, JACOB BERNARD (Columbia, 1902) *Corneille and the Spanish drama.* New York. The Col. Univ. press, 1902. ix, 147 p. 2-19594

SELBERT, LOUIS (Yale, 1916) **A glossary of Juan Manuel's El Libro de los Enxiemplos del Conde Lucanor et de Patronio.* [Deceased.]

†SERONDE, JOSEPH (Yale, 1915) **A study of the relations of some leading French poets of the fourteenth and fifteenth centuries to the Marqués de Santillana.*

†SEYMOUR, ARTHUR ROMEYN (Wisconsin, 1907)

The development in Spanish of the Latin pluperfect indicative.

†SHANKS, LEWIS EDGAR PIAGET (Cornell, 1908) *The marvelous and the fantastic in the French romantic novel.*

SHAPIRO, ALBERT ABRAHAM (Harvard 1916) *The Libertins in France in the seventeenth century.*

†SHAW, JAMES EUSTACE (Johns Hopkins, 1900) *The use of "venire" and "andare" as auxiliary verbs in early Florentine prose.* Part I. Baltimore, J. Murphy co., 1903. 42 p. 11-2328

SHEFLOE, JOSEPH SAMUEL (Johns Hopkins, 1890) *Observations on the phonology and inflections of the Jersey French Dialect.*

†SHELLY, PERCY VAN DYKE (Pennsylvania, 1914) ...*English and French in England, 1066-1100.* Philadelphia, Pa., 1921. 97 p. 22-3244

†SHERWOOD, MARGARET MERRIAM (Columbia, 1918) *La vie de Saint Brendan.* Critical ed. made on facsimiles of the original MSS.

†SHULTERS, JOHN RAYMOND (Illinois, 1918) *Luigi Pulci and the animal kingdom...* Baltimore, J. H. Furst company, 1920. 3 p. l., 118 p. 20-19530

SIMS, ELMER RICHARD (Chicago, 1926) *La segunda parte de La Vida de Lazarillo de Tormes. Sacada de las crónicas antiguas de Toledo. Por I. De Luna Castellano, intérprete de la lengua española.*

†SIRICH, EDWARD HINMAN (Johns Hopkins, 1914) *A study in the syntax of Alexandre Hardy...* Baltimore, J. H. Furst company, 1915. 32 p. 15-23427

†SMEAD, JANE VAN NESS (Johns Hopkins, 1921)

Chateaubriand et la Bible. Baltimore, The Johns Hopkins press; etc., 1924. 44 p. ["Part of a larger publ., which will appear as the second vol. of the J. H. U. series in Romance lits. et langs."] 24-19787 [Pub. 1924. 166 p.]

†SMITH, HELEN BELLE (Wisconsin, 1925) *The skepticism of Anatole France.* [Pub. 1927. 186 p.]

†SMITH, HORATIO ELWIN (Johns Hopkins, 1912) *The literary criticism of Pierre Bayle...* Albany, N. Y., The Brandow printing co., 1912. 135 p. 12-32045

†SMITH, PETER FRANK, JR. (Chicago, 1924) *"Esta es la translación del psalterio que fizo maestro Herman el aleman, segund cuemo esta en el ebraygo."* Reprint of the only extant MS., Escor. ij. 8, with introd. and notes. [Ed. R. M. M. Have been unable to obtain publication data.]

†SMITH, ROBERT METCALF (Columbia, 1915) *Froissart and the English chronicle play...* New York, Col. Univ. press, 1915. xiii, 165 p. [Col. Univ. stud. in Eng. and compar. lit.] 16-6431

†SMITH, WINIFRED (Columbia, 1912) *The commedia dell'arte; a study in Italian popular comedy...* New York, 1912. xv, 291 p. [Col. Univ. stud. in Eng. and compar. lit. v. 2.] [Appendix A: Scenarios; Appendix B: Relations between English and Italian drama in the 16th, 17th and 18th centuries.] 13-1262

†SNAVELY, GUY EVERETT (Johns Hopkins, 1908) [ed.]... *The Aesopic fables in the Mireoir historical of Jehan de Vignay.* Ed. with introd., notes, bibliog. Balto., 1908. 47 p. 8-20857

†SPAULDING, ROBERT KILBURN (California, 1925) **A study of the history and syntax of progressive constructions in Spanish.*

†SPIERS, ALEXANDER GUY HOLBORN (Harvard, 1909) *The character and effectiveness of final lines in Dante's lyric.

†SPIKER, CLAUDE CARL (Chicago, 1922) *The historical development of the cesura in the French decasyllable.

†SPRING, HENRY POWELL (Columbia, 1924) Chateaubriand at the crossways; a character study analyzing the non-literary sources of Chateaubriand's opinions as expressed in the Essai sur les révolutions. New York, Col. Univ. press. 1924. xix, 195 p. 24-29896

†STAAF, OSCAR EMIL (Yale, 1907) *Classical mythology in Calderón.

STALEY, ETHEL MAY (Johns Hopkins, 1926) *George Sand and Jean-Jacques Rousseau.

†STANSBURY, MILTON HAMMOND (Pennsylvania, 1926) Foreign languages and interpreters in the Old-French chansons de geste. [Univ. of Pa. Series in Romanic langs. and lits., No. 18.] [In press.]

STODDARD, THEODORE LOTHROP (Harvard, 1914) The French revolution in San Domingo... Boston and New York, Houghton Mifflin company, 1914. xviii, 410 p. 14-20788 [Dept. Hist.]

†STORER, WALTER HENRY (Illinois, 1922) Virgil and Ronsard. Paris, E. Champion, 1923. xviii, 143 p. 24-8278

STOWELL, WILLIAM AVERILL (Johns Hopkins, 1908) Old-French titles of respect in direct address. Balto., 1908. xiv. 237 p. 8-21808

†STUART, DONALD CLIVE (Columbia, 1910) Stage decoration in France in the Middle Ages. New York, The Columbia Univ. press, 1910. 12mo., ix, 230 p. 10-11547

†STURDEVANT, WINIFRED (Johns Hopkins, 1920) *The Misterio de los Reyes Magos: its position in the development of the mediaeval legend of the three kings.*

SWANN, HARVEY JULIAN (Columbia, 1918) *French terminologies in the making; studies in conscious contributions to the vocabulary...* New York, Col. Univ. press, 1918. xxii, 250 p. [Half-title: Col. Univ. stud. in Romance philol. and lit.] 19-6717

SWITZER, REBECCA (Columbia, 1927) *The Ciceronian style of fray Luis de Granada.* [To be published, summer 1927. Col. Univ. press, circa 150 p.]

SYLVANIA, LENA EVELYN VINCENT (Columbia, 1922) *Doña María de Zayas y Sotomayor; a contribution to the study of her works.* New York, Col. Univ. press, 1922. ix, 52 p. [Half-title: Col. Univ. stud. in Romance philol. and lit.] [A part of a work now in preparation. Cf. Pref.] 22-14303

SYMINGTON, WILLIAM STUART (Johns Hopkins, 1895) *The folk-lore of May-day in France.* [Deceased, 1926.]

†TARR, FREDERICK COURTNEY (Princeton, 1921) *Prepositional complementary clauses in Spanish, with special reference to the works of Pérez Galdós.* New York, Paris, 1922. 2 p. l., 264 p., 1l. ["Extrait de la Revue hispanique, tome, LVI".] 24-14623

†TAYLOR, PAULINE (Columbia, 1924) *The Latinity of the Liber Historiae Francorum.* New York, 1924. 142 p. 25-5208

TAYLOR, ROBERT LONGLEY (Yale, 1900) *Alliteration in Italian.* New Haven, Conn., The Tuttle, Morehouse and Taylor co., 1900. 151 p. [Deceased, May 27, 1923.] 19-16997

†TEMPLE, MAUD ELIZ., (Radcliffe, 1913) *Christine de Pisan and the Victorine revival.*

†TEMPLIN, ERNEST HALL (Stanford, 1927) *The Carolingian tradition in the Spanish drama of the Golden Age, (excluding Lope de Vega).* 358 p.

†THIEME, HUGO PAUL (Johns Hopkins, 1897) *The technique of the French Alexandrine. A study of the works of Leconte de Lisle, José María de Hérédia, François Coppée, Sully-Prudhomme, and Paul Verlaine.* Ann Arbor, 1877. 68 p. 12-28818

†THORNTON, HEMAN HERVEY (Chicago, 1925) *An edition of the poems ascribed to the Emperor Frederick II and his sons.*

†TISDEL, FREDERICK MONROE (Harvard, 1900) *Comedy in the mystery plays of England, France and Germany.* Pub. in part, with modifications, as "The influence of popular customs on the mystery plays", in Journ. Eng. and Germ. philol., 1904. v: 323-340 p. [Dept. Eng. lit.]

†TITCHENER, FRANCES HALIBURTON (Radcliffe, 1925) *La renaissance méridionale dans la province d'Auvergne.*

†TITSWORTH, PAUL EMERSON (Wisconsin, 1911) *The attitude of Goethe and Schiller toward the French classic drama.* [In the Journ. of Eng. and Germ. philol. October, 1912. Urbana, Ill. 1912. vol. xi, no. 4. 509-564 p.] [A limited number of copies reprinted.] 13-4096-7

TODD, HENRY ALFRED (Johns Hopkins, 1885) *Le Dit de la panthère d'amours par Nicole de Margival; poème du XIIIᵉ S., publié d'après les MSS. de Paris et de Saint-Pétersbourg.* Paris, Firmin-Didot et cie., 1883. xxxix, 115 p. [Soc. des Anc. Textes fr.] [Deceased, 1925.]

†TORREY, NORMAN LEWIS (Harvard, 1926) *The English critical deists and their influence on Voltaire.*

†TOWLES, OLIVER (Johns Hopkins, 1912) *Prepositional phrases of asseveration and adjuration in Old and Middle French.* Paris, E. Champion, 1920. x, 156 p., 2l. 20-17236

†TRAUTMAN, WILLIAM DANIEL (Chicago, 1923) *An edition of the prologue and théophile of Gautier de Coincy's miracles de la Sainte Vierge.*

TROTAIN, MARTHE (Bryn Mawr, 1921) *Les scènes historiques, étude du théâtre livresque à la veille du drame romantique.* Paris, E. Champion, 1923. 73p., 4o., 1l. 24-5128

†TURVILLE, DOROTHY (Columbia, 1925) *French feminine singular nouns derived from Latin neuter plurals.* New York, Col. Univ. press, 1925. 236 p. 25-15085

TYLER, ELIZABETH STEARNS (Columbia, 1918) *La Chaçun de Willame: An edition of the unique manuscript of the poem with vocabulary and a table of proper nouns.* New York, Oxford Univ. press, 1919. xvii, 173 p. [Deceased.]

†UMPHREY, GEORGE WALLACE (Harvard, 1905) *A study of the Aragonese dialect, based on a fourteenth century manuscript, now edited for the first time.* Pub. in two parts, as "Aragonese texts," in the Revue hispanique, 1907. xvi, p. 244-287; and the "Aragonese dialect", ibid., 1911. xxiv, p. 5-45.

UNDERHILL, JOHN GARRETT (Columbia, 1899) *Spanish literature in the England of the Tudors.* New York, Col. Univ. press. 1899. x, 438 p. A11-994

†UNDERWOOD, CHARLES MARSHALL (Harvard,

1905) *The ars poetica of the sweet new style: a study of the second book of Dante's treatise De Vulgati Eloquentia and of its relation to certain early Italian canzoni.

†UNDERWOOD, GEORGE ARTHUR (Harvard, 1914) *Rousseauism in the works of Madame de Staël.* Results pub. as "Rousseauism in two early works of Madame de Staël". Mod. philol., 1915. xiii: 417-432 p.

†VAETH, JOSEPH ANTHONY (Columbia, 1918) *Tirant lo Blanch; a study of its authorship, principal sources and historical setting...* New York, Col. Univ. press. 1918. xvi, 169 p. 1l. [Half-title: Col. Univ. stud. in Romance philol. and lit.] 19-6030

†VAILLANT, RENÉ E. G. (Columbia, 1926) *Concepción Arenal.* New York. Instituto de las Españas en los E. U., 1926. [Preface I. Introd. II. 15-160 p. Notes and Bibliog. 161-192 p.]

†VAN HORNE, JOHN (Harvard, 1913) *The relation of Giacomo Leopardi to classical antiquity.* Results pub. as "Studies on Leopardi". Univ. Iowa. Humanistic stud., I: no. 4, 1916. 1-31 p. [Dept. compar. lit.]

†VÁSQUEZ-ARJONA, CARLOS (Johns Hopkins, 1925) *Cotejo histórico de cinco episodios de Galdós.*

†VAUGHAN, HERBERT HUNTER (Harvard, 1906) *The language of Il Fiore.*

VENTURA, MIGUEL (Cornell, 1909) *Historical Catalan phonetics.*

†VERMONT, ADOLPHE (Johns Hopkins, 1924) *Les amis français de Franklin.*

†VEXLER, FELIX (Columbia, 1922) *Studies in Di-*

derot's esthetic naturalism. New York, 1922. 115 p. 21. 22-19325

†WADE, IRA OWEN (Princeton, 1924) *The "philosophe" in the French drama of the eighteenth century.* Princeton and Paris, 1926. xi, 143 p. [Elliott monographs, no. 18.] 26-18430

†WAGNER, CHARLES PHILIP (Yale, 1902) *The sources of El Cavallero Cifar.* Pub. in slightly different form, in the Revue hispanique, 1903. X, 5-104 p.

†WALES, JULIA GRACE (Wisconsin, 1926) *English and Italian elements in five Italian plays of Shakespeare.*

WALKER, JOHN CHARLES (Cornell, 1898) *Characteristics of French syntax of the 16th century as exemplified in the language of Marguerite of Navarre.*

†WARD, CHARLES FREDERICK (Chicago, 1911) *The Epistles on the "Romance of the Rose" and other documents in the debate.* Toronto, 1911. 117 p. 13-22789

†WARE, JOHN NOTTINGHAM (Johns Hopkins, 1924) *The vocabulary of Bernardin de Saint-Pierre and its relation to the French romantic school.*

†WARREN, FREDERICK MORRIS (Johns Hopkins, 1887) *The world of Corneille. A study of popular movements and notions as seen in his works.*

†WATERHOUSE, FRANCIS ASBURY (Harvard, 1918) *Sedaine the librettist.*

WAXMEN, SAMUEL MONTEFIORE (Harvard, 1912) *Chapters on magic in Spanish literature.* Pub. in the Revue hispanique, 1916. XXXVIII, 325-463 p.

†WEBSTER, KENNETH GRANT TREMAYNE (Har-

vard, 1902) *Lancelot and Guinevere: a study
in the origins of Arthurian romance.* A por-
tion condensed, pub. as "Arthur and Charlemagne", in Englishe Studien, 1906. XXXVI,
337-369 p. [Dept. Eng. lit.]

†WEDEL, THEODORE OTTO (Yale, 1918) *The mediaeval attitude toward astrology, particularly
in England...* New Haven, Yale Univ. press;
[etc., etc.] 1920. v p., 1l., 163 p. [Yale studies
in English. A. S. Cook, editor, LX.] 20-14391

†WEEKS, RAYMOND (Harvard, 1897) *Aliscans and
Nerbonesi.* Results, revised, pub. as "The prim-
itive Prise d'Orange," in PMLA, 1901. xvi,
p, 361-374; "Etudes sur Aliscans," in Romania,
1901. xxx, p. 184-197; 1905. xxxiv, p. 237-277;
1909. xxxviii, p. 1-43; and "Origin of the Co-
venant Vivien", in Univ. of Missouri stud., I,
Columbia, Mo., 1902. 8ᵛᵒ., viii, 64 p.

†WESENBERG, THOR GRIFFITH (Harvard, 1925)
**A study of the conditional and the subjunc-
tive in Provençal narrative poetry.*

WEST, ROBERT WILLIAM (Wisconsin, 1926) **The
nature of vocal sounds.*

†WHITE, FLORENCE DONNELL (Bryn Mawr, 1915)
*Voltaire's Essay on epic poetry; a study and
an edition... by Florence Donnell White...*
Albany, N.Y., The Brandow printing co., 1915.
vii, 167 p. 16-4410

†WHITMAN, IRIS LILIAN (Columbia, 1927) *Longfellow and Spain.* [In press.]

†WHITMORE, CHARLES EDWARD (Harvard, 1911)
The supernatural in tragedy... Cambridge,
Harv. Univ. press; [etc., etc.] 1915. viii, 370 p.
16-2250 [Dept. compar. lit.]

†WHITNEY, MARIAN PARKER (Yale, 1901) **The*

young King and largesse. A study in medieval manners.

†WHITTEM, ARTHUR FISHER (Harvard, 1908)
*The sources of the fables in Juan Ruiz's Libro de Buen Amor.

†WIGHTMAN, JOHN ROAF (Johns Hopkins, 1888)
*The French language in Canada.

†WILKINS, ERNEST HATCH (Harvard, 1910) *The chronology of the youth of Boccaccio.* Two chapters pub. as "The date of the birth of Boccaccio" in the Romanic review, 1910. I, p. 367-373; and "The enamorment of Boccaccio" in Modern philology, 1913. xi, p. 39-55.

†WILL, JOSEPH STANLEY (Columbia, 1921) *Protestantism in France. Volume two, 1598-1629...* [Toronto] Univ. of Toronto press, 1921. 4 p. l., 7-265, [5] p. [The complete work, which is to consist of 3 vols, has not yet been published. cf. Preface.] 22-4192

†WILLIAMS, EDWIN BUCHER (Pennsylvania, 1924) *The life and dramatic works of Gertrudis Gómez de Avellaneda.* Phila., 1924. 116 p. [On cover. Univ. of Pa. publs. Series in Romanic langs. and lits. II.] 24-15204

WILLIAMS, GRACE SARA (Columbia, 1907) *The "Amadis" question.* Pub. in the Revue hispanique, xxi, Paris, 1909. iii, 168 p.

†WILLIAMS, RALPH COPLESTONE (Johns Hopkins, 1917) *The theory of the heroic epic in Italian criticism of the sixteenth century...* [Baltimore, 1921] vi, 22 p. 1l. 21-8203

†WILSON, JAMES HERBERT (Wisconsin, 1921) **La vie poétique de Guillaume d'Orange.* [No. Ms.]

WILSON, RICHARD HENRY (Johns Hopkins, 1898) *The preposition à. The relation of its meanings studied in Old-French. Part I. Situation.*

Baltimore, 1902. viii, 77 p. [Printed dissertation issue contains one part only.]

†WINFREY, LEWIS EDGAR (Chicago, 1925) *The courtly elements in Eilhart von Oberge's Tristrant, Part I.*

†WISEWELL, GEORGE ELLAS (Wisconsin, 1919) *Finite moods and tenses in the Don Quijote of Cervantes.*

†WITHERS, ALFRED MILES (Pennsylvania, 1923) *The sources of the poetry of Gutierre de Cetina.* Philadelphia, Pa., Printed by Westbrook publishing co., 1923. 91 p. [On cover: Univ. of Pa. publications. Series in Romanic langs. and lits. no. 9.] 24-4890

†WITHERS, VIRGINIA REESE (Chicago, 1926) *American types in French drama from the American revolution through the world war.*

WOLLSTEIN, ROSE HEYLBUT (Columbia, 1923) *English opinions of French poetry, 1660-1750.* New York, Col. Univ. press, 1923. xi, 103 p., 1l. [Half-title: Col. Univ. stud. in Romance philol. and lit.] 23-11066

†WOOD, GEORGE CAMPBELL (Harvard, 1920) *The questions of love in mediaeval French literature as a reflection of social conditions.*

WOOD, MARY MORTON (Columbia, 1917) *The spirit of protest in Old French literature...* New York. Col. Univ. press, 1917. xii, 201 p. 1l. [Half-title: Col. Univ. stud. in Romance philol. and lit.] 17-31157

†WOODBRIDGE, BENJAMIN MATHER (Harvard, 1913) *La vie et les oeuvres de Gatien de Courtilz, Sieur du Verger.* Résumé of part pub. as "Gatien de Courtilz, Sieur du Verger, a precursor of Lesage" in Mod. lang. rev. 1914. ix, p. 475-492. Pub. as "Gatien de Courtilz,

Sieur du Verger, étude sur un Précurseur du Roman réaliste en France," Johns Hopkins stud. in Rom. lit. and lang., 1925. vol. VI, 226 p. [Pub. also by Les presses universitaires de France.]

†YOUNG, CHARLES EDMUND (Wisconsin, 1912) *The marriage question in the modern French drama (1850-1911)* [Philol. and lit. Series of the Bulletin of the Univ. of Wis. Madison. vol. 5, no. 4, 1915, 93 p.]

†ZAPATA Y TORRES, MIGUEL (Cornell, 1926) *El Libro del consejo e los consejeros; por Maestro Pedro.*

†ZDANOWICZ, CASIMIR DOUGLAS (Harvard, 1906) *Greek proper names in Old French.*

TOPICAL INDEX

Acadian dialect,
    See Geddes.
Aesopic fable,
    See Harry,
       Snavely.
Alexander,
    See Miller.
Aliscans,
    See Weeks.
Aljamiado texts,
    See Nykl.
Allegory,
    See Jodocius,
      Post.
Alliance,
    See Cresson.
Alliteration,
    See Krappe,
      Taylor.
Amadas et Ydoine,
    See Reinhard.
Amadis de Gaula,
    See Williams.
American Alliance of 1778,
    See Corwin.
American education,
    See Gager.
American literature,
    See Ferguson,
      Mantz.
American magazines,
    See Cool.
American travellers,
    See Farnham.
Animal kingdom,
    See Garver,
      Holbrook,
      Shulters.
Archaisms,
    See Colin.
Aristotelians (French),
    See Dutton,
      McPike.

Arthurian material,
    See Fisher,
      Fletcher,
      Hill,
      Hopkins,
      Lister,
      Nitze,
      Webster.
Astrology,
    See Wedel.
Aymeri de Narbonne,
    See Crabb.
Ballade, The,
    See Cohen.
Barbier de Seville,
    See Jones.
Basque,
    See Redfield.
Bestiary and Lapidary,
    See Rice.
Bourgeois, The
    See Peirce.
Bouillon family,
    See Galland.
Brendan (vie de Saint)
    See Sherwood.
Brut,
    See Gillespy.
Canada,
    See Wightman.
Catalan,
    See Bourland,
      Heaton,
      Ventura.
Chaçun de Willame,
    See Tyler,
      Hamilton.
Chansons de geste,
    See Comfort,
      Crabb,
      Dickman,
      Farnsworth,
      Stansbury.

Charlemagne,
    See Webster.
Charles de Sainte-Marthe
    (Trans. into French by
    Marcel Bonnet),
        See Ruutz-Rees.
Child, The defense of the
    See Parker.
Cid, Poema del,
    See Coester,
        Rogers.
Cifar, El Cavallero,
    See Wagner.
Colour,
    See Levengood,
Comédie-vaudeville,
    See Arvin,
        Bruerton.
Commedia dell'arte,
    See Smith.
Decameron,
    See Child.
Devil, The,
    See Degeler,
        Rudwin.
Divine comedy,
    See Dante.
Don Quixote (See Cervan-
    tes),
        See Brownell,
            Corley,
            Gould,
            Wisewell.
Dreyfus affair,
    See Jordon.
Edmond (vie de saint),
    See Haxo,
        Leftwich.
English influences,
    See Churchman,
        Cru,
        Myrick,
        Torrey.
English novel,
    See Gregory,
        Huffman.
English opinions,
    See Woolstein.

English poets,
    See Halley,
        Hancock.
English stage,
    See Bruce,
        McLeod.
European characters,
    See Kurz.
Exoticism,
    See Atkinson,
        Malakis,
        Schwartz.
Fabliaux,
    See Herrick.
Fiore (Il),
    See Vaughan.
Folk-lore,
    See Symington.
French Assembly of 1848,
    See Curtis.
French criticism,
    See Conrad,
        Gager,
        Mantz.
French drama,
    See Acton,
        Aldrich,
        Bernbaum,
        Bissell,
        Brenner,
        Cattell,
        De Vries,
        Hubert,
        Jones,
        Kurz,
        Lamouret,
        Lancaster,
        Langer,
        Long,
        McMahon,
        Mason,
        Norman,
        Patch,
        Porter,
        Ross,
        Rougier,
        Schoenberger,
        Stuart,
        Titsworth,

Trotain,
Wade,
Withers,
Young.
French epic,
    See Fundenburg,
        Potter,
        White.
French epistle,
    See Parmenter.
French influences,
    See Havens,
        McLeod,
        Pflueger,
        Seronde,
        Smith.
French novel,
    See De Vries,
        Hornicek,
        Hubert,
        Huffman,
        Kany,
        Parker,
        Shanks.
French Protestantism,
    See Kelly,
        Will.
French Revolution,
    See Gregory,
        Hancock,
        Hardy,
        Reiff,
        Stoddard.
French versification,
    See Dondo,
        Hudson,
        Parmenter,
        Spiker,
        Thieme,
        Wollstein.
Genoese,
    See Byrne.
Godefroi de Bouillon,
    See Fite.
Gongorism,
    See Kane.
Grotesque (See Quevedo),
    See Freeman,
        Rose.

Guernsey,
    See Lewis.
Gui de Bourgoyne,
    See Cipriani.
Gui de Cambrai,
    See Edwards.
Guillaume d'Angleterre,
    See Ogden.
Guillaume d'Orange,
    See Wilson.
d'Haveloc, Lai
    See Fahnestock
Henry Plantagenet,
    See Moore.
Heptameron (See Marguerite
    de Navarre),
    See Lamb.
Hubiera and *hubiese,*
    See Hatheway.
Idylls of fishermen,
    See Hall.
Ipomedon,
    See Carter.
Isopo laurenziano,
    See Brush.
Italian borrowings,
    See Myrick.
Italian criticism,
    See Williams.
Italian drama,
    See Smith.
Italian influences,
    See Boecker,
        Camera,
        Di Santo,
        Goggio,
        Halley,
        Hamilton,
        Pirazzini,
        Post,
        Smith,
        Wales.
Italian poetry,
    See Baxter,
        Bullock,
        Garver,
        Livingston,
        McKenzie,
        Moseley,

Mott,
Spiers,
Taylor,
Underwood,
Vaughan.
Jean de Crèvecoeur, Saint,
See Mitchell.
Jeux floraux,
See Dawson.
Labor movement in France,
See Levine.
Language,
See Brandenburg,
Roumiguière,
Shelly,
West,
Wightman.
Latin,
See Anderson,
Armstrong,
Barry,
Bartlett,
Clark,
Colbert,
Delamarre,
Guyer,
Jodocius,
Lhevinne,
Parker,
Raggio,
Redfield,
Rice,
Rougier,
Taylor.
Lazarillo de Tormes,
See Sims.
Libertins, The,
See Shapiro.
Libro del Consejo,
See Zapata y Torres.
Libro de Buen Amor,
See Richardson,
Whittem.
Libro de los gatos,
See Northup.
Literary criticism,
See Hutchings,
Lacombe,
Lamouret,

Lansing,
McLeod,
McMahon,
Olmsted,
Patch,
Patzer,
Pierce,
Pélissier,
Pirazzini,
Porter,
Seronde,
Smith,
Wollstein.
Literary patronage,
See Holzknecht.
Magos, de los Reyes,
See Sturdevant.
Marriage,
See Young.
Martín Fierro (an Epic of
the Argentine),
See Holmes.
Mediaeval life,
See Crane,
Dana,
Fundenburg,
Herrick,
Porter,
Stuart,
Sturdevant,
Whitney,
Wood.
Mediaeval visions,
See Dana.
Mer, La,
See Ditchy.
Mesta, The,
See Klein.
Mexico,
See Barranco.
Marden.
Phipps.
Miracles,
See Grundler,
Trautman.
Monroe Doctrine,
See Cresson,
Méras.

Moors,
    See Dale,
      Deferrari.
Mystery play,
    See Carnahan,
      Tisdel.
Mystic vision,
    See Fisher.
Naimon de Bavière,
    See Michell.
Negro question,
    See Hardy.
New Mexican Spanish,
    See Espinosa,
      Hills.
Nostradamus,
    See Parker.
Novela picaresca,
    See picaresque novel.
Old-French,
    See Allen,
      Armstrong,
      Barrow,
      Brush,
      Carnahan,
      Cerf,
      Clarke,
      Critchlow,
      Curdy,
      Davidson,
      Dedecek,
      Degeler,
      Dickman,
      Edwards,
      Fahnestock,
      Farnsworth,
      Fisher,
      Fite,
      Fletcher,
      Galpin,
      Gillespy,
      Goddard,
      Grundler,
      Haxo,
      Holzknecht,
      House,
      Jenkins,
      Jones,
      Keidel,

      Krappe,
      Lodeman,
      Lowe,
      Luquiens,
      McKibben,
      Michell,
      Molenaer,
      Morrison,
      Neff,
      Nitze,
      Ogden,
      Ostrander,
      Porter,
      Reinhard,
      Robbins,
      Ruutz-Rees,
      Seronde,
      Shelly,
      Sherwood,
      Stowell,
      Todd,
      Trautman,
      Tyler,
      Vaeth,
      Ward,
      Webster,
      Weeks,
      Wilson,
      Wood (twice),
      Zdanowicz.
Old-Italian,
    See Altrocchi,
      Carnahan,
      Ettari,
      Garver,
      Grimm.
Old-Provençal,
    See Brinsmade,
      Galpin.
Old-Spanish,
    See Beardsley,
      De Forest,
      English,
      Fitz-Gerald,
      Frost,
      Luquiens,
      Mackenzie,
      Miller,
      Northup,

Nykl,
Sims,
Smith,
Sturdevant,
Umphrey,
Wagner.
Othello,
   See Gilman.
Paris Psalter,
   See Bartlett.
Pathelin, Maistre Pierre,
   See Patrick.
Perlesvaus,
   See Lister,
     Nitze.
Philology, French,
   See Alexander,
     Andison,
     Bergeron,
     Béziat de Bordes,
     Blondheim,
     Bonnotte,
     DeForest,
     Dey,
     Fay,
     Frein,
     Gerig,
     Gill,
     Hacker,
     Holmes,
     Hudson,
     Jagemann,
     Knickerbocker,
     Krappe,
     Kuersteiner,
     Laubscher,
     Levy,
     Livingston,
     Luker,
     Mathews,
     Matzke,
     Menut,
     Muller,
     Patrick,
     Poyen-Bellisle,
     Shelly,
     Sirich,
     Spiker,
     Stowell,

Swann,
Towles,
Turville,
Walker,
Wilson.
Philology, Italian,
   See Baxter,
     Brown,
     Bruner,
     Child,
     Clark,
     Field,
     Goggio,
     Gruenbaum,
     Johnson,
     McCabe,
     Menger,
     Salvio,
     Schlatter,
     Shaw,
     Spiers,
     Taylor.
Philology, Romance,
   See Arnold,
     Bowen,
     Buckingham,
     Fay,
     Fontaine,
     Garner,
     Gerig,
     Redfield.
Philology, Spanish,
   See Bailiff,
     Beardsley,
     Brownell,
     Chenery,
     Cheskis,
     Corley,
     DeForest,
     English,
     Fitz-Gerald,
     Ford,
     Gordon,
     Gould,
     Henríquez Ureña,
     Hill,
     Meredith,
     Moore,
     O'Connor,

Raggio,
Reed,
Rogers,
Seymour,
Spaulding,
Sturdevant,
Tarr,
Umphrey,
Wisewell.
Phonology,
　　See Bruner,
　　　Ford,
　　　Frein,
　　　Logie,
　　　Marden,
　　　Matzke,
　　　Rice,
　　　Shefloe.
Picaresque novel,
　　See Chandler,
　　　De Haan,
　　　Eveleth.
Platonic theories,
　　See Kerr,
　　　Merrill.
Pléiade, La,
　　See Levengood.
Protestantism,
　　See Will.
Provençal, Modern,
　　See Adams,
　　　Ford,
　　　Wesenberg.
Puy, The,
　　See Patterson.
Quotidienne, la,
　　See King.
Relations internationales,
　　See Roumiguière.
Relations of poetry to industry,
　　See Grant.
Renaissance,
　　See Hyma,
　　　Kerr,
　　　Titchener.
Romans bretons,
　　See Easter.

Romans d'aventure,
　　See Critchlow,
　　　Easter,
　　　Morrison.
Roman de la Rose,
　　See Fansler,
　　　Luquiens,
　　　Ward.
Roman de la Violette,
　　See Buffum,
　　　Lowe.
Romans dou lis,
　　See Ostrander.
Romanticism,
　　See Hagboldt,
　　　Heller,
　　　Ware.
Roumanian Poetry,
　　See Feraru.
Saint Alexius,
　　See Altrocchi.
Saint Nicholas,
　　See Crawford.
Salammbô,
　　See Blossom,
　　　Hamilton.
Semantics,
　　See Gerig,
　　　Menut.
Siete Partidas,
　　See Edgerly.
Sonnet,
　　See Bullock,
　　　Olmstead.
Spanish Drama,
　　See Dale,
　　　Goldberg,
　　　Hendrix,
　　　Jack,
　　　Martell,
　　　Meredith,
　　　Segall,
　　　Templin.
Spanish influences,
　　See Beckmann,
　　　Crooks,
　　　Morley,
　　　Underhill,
　　　Whitman.

Spanish inns,
  See Farnham.
Spanish poetry,
  See Gordon,
    Henríquez Ureña,
    Mann.
Stage decoration,
  See Stuart.
Stichomythia,
  See Hancock.
Supernatural,
  See Calcott,
    Dickman,
    Easter,
    Kahn,
    Rudwin,
    Shanks,
    Waxmen,
    Whitmore.
Symbolism,
  See Price.

Tirant Lo Blanch,
  See Vaeth.
Toulouse,
  See Dawson.
Transcendantalisme,
  See Girard.
Treatment of women,
  See Lansing,
    Neff.
Tristran,
  See Curdy,
    Winfrey.
Troilus and Criseyde,
  See Hamilton.
Uncle and Nephew,
  See Farnsworth.
Vers libre,
  See Dondo.
Women's costume,
  See Goddard.

ROMANCE AUTHORS' INDEX

Adenet Le Roi,
  See Davidson.
Alfonso X, el Sabio,
  See Calcott,
    Dexter,
    Edgerly.
Ambrose, Saint,
  See Barry.
Ariosto,
  See Dunn,
    McMurphy.
Aristotle,
  See Dutton,
    McPike.
Augustine, Saint,
  See Barry,
    Colbert.
Avellaneda, Gertrudis Gómez
  de,
  See Williams.
Arenal, Concepción,
  See Vaillant.

Baïf, Antoine de,
  See Ingraham.
Balzac, Honoré de,
  See Burton,
    Fess,
    Floyd,
    Garnand,
    Hastings,
    Preston.
Baudelaire,
  See Rhodes.
Bayle, Pierre,
  See Smith.
Beaulieu, Eustorg de (A disciple of Marot),
  See Harvitt.
Beauvais, Pierre de (XIIIe S.),
  See Fisher.
Bellay, Joachim du,
  See Merrill.
Berceo, Gonzalo de,
  See Fitz-Gerald.

Bergson,
 See Peckham,
  Landes,
  Mrs. Sait.
Bertrand, Louis,
 See Cabeen.
Boccaccio,
 See Bourland,
  Cummings,
  Wilkins.
Boileau,
 See Clark,
  Miller.
Boissy, Louis de,
 See Constans.
Bourget, Paul,
 See Bowman.
Boutroux, Emile,
 See Crawford.
Bozon, Nicole,
 See Harry.
Brieux,
 See Scheifley.
Byron,
 See Churchman.
Caballero, Ferán
 See Hespelt.
Calderón de la Barca, D. Pe-
 dro,
  See Castillo,
  Rosenberg,
  Staaf.
Carducci,
 See Sbedico.
Castillejo, Cristóbal de
 See Nicolay.
Cecco d'Ascoli,
 See Rice.
Cervantes (See Don Quixo-
 te),
  See Crooks.
Cetina, Gutierre de
 See Withers.
Charron, Pierre
 See Bergeron.
Chateaubriand,
 See Miller,
  Naylor,
  Rudwin,

  Smead,
  Spring.
Chaucer,
 See Cummings,
  Fansler,
  Hamilton,
  Jones.
Chrétien de Troyes,
 See Guyer,
  Hopkins,
  Little.
Christine de Pizan,
 See Babcock,
  Laigle,
  Temple.
Colletet, Guillaume,
 See de Boer.
Colonne, Guido delle
 See Hamilton.
Corneille,
 See Aldrich,
  Barney,
  Canfield,
  McPike,
  Mallarian,
  Riddle,
  van Roosbroeck,
  Segall,
  Warren.
Cottin, Mme.,
 See Hornicek.
Dante,
 See Field,
  Fisher,
  Halley,
  Holbrook,
  Mott,
  Murray,
  Post,
  Rolbiecki,
  Salvio,
  Spiers,
  Underwood.
Da Ponte, Lorenzo,
 See Russo.
Denis Piramus or *Pyramus,*
 See Haxo,
  Leftwich.
  Sherwood.

Descartes,
    See Kahn.
Deschamps, Eustache,
    See Patzer.
Diderot,
    See Cru,
        Vexler.
Dumas, fils.,
    See Schwarz.
Durkheim, Emile,
    See Gehlke.
Echegaray, Don José,
    See Goldberg.
Edmund, Saint,
    See Robbins.
Eichendorff,
    See Beckmann.
Eilhart d'Oberg,
    See Winfrey.
Fabre, Ferdinand,
    See Bowen.
Feydeau, Ernest,
    See Noble.
Flaubert,
    See Blossom,
        Coleman,
        Hamilton,
        Riddell.
Fontaine, Maître Charles,
    See Hawkins.
Frederick II,
    See Thornton.
France, Anatole,
    See Smith.
Franklin,
    See Vermont.
Froissart,
    See Smith.
Fromentin, Eugène,
    See Ives.
Furetière, Antoine,
    See Bronk.
Galdós, Pérez,
    See Tarr,
        Vásquez-Arjona.
Gálvez, José de,
    See Priestley.
Garcilaso de la Vega,
    See Keniston.

Gatien de Courtilz,
    See Woodbridge.
Gautier d'Arras,
    See Cowper.
Gautier de Coinci,
    See Trautman.
Gautier, Théophile,
    See Patch.
Giacomo da Lentino,
    See Langley.
Godfroi de Bouillon,
    See Fite,
        Galland.
Gontier Col,
    See Le Duc.
Gourmont, Remy de
    See Crawford.
Granada, fray Luis de,
    See Switzer.
Grimm, F. M.,
    See Jones.
Guérin de (or du) Bouscal,
    See Crooks.
Guillén de Castro (1569-
    1630),
        See Alpern,
        Hyman.
Gutiérrez, García,
    See Adams.
Hardy, Alexandre,
    See Sirich.
Hermosilla, Diego de,
    See Mackenzie.
Herrera, Fernando de,
    See Beach.
Hervieu, Paul,
    See Hubert.
d'Holbach, Baron,
    See Cushing.
Hugo, Victor,
    See Ditchy,
        Freeman,
        Schenck.
Hume, David,
    See Doxsee,
        Peoples.
Ibáñez, Blasco,
    See Gilbert.

Ibsen, French criticism of,
        See Conrad.
Isidore of Seville,
        See Brehaut.
Jehan de Tuim (or *Tuin*),
        See Dedecek.
Jehan de Vignay,
        See Snavely.
Juan Manuel,
        See Rockwood,
            Selbert.
Juan Ruiz,
        See Richardson,
            Whittem.
La Fontaine,
        See Fischer.
Lamartine,
        See Pirazzini.
Leconte de Lisle,
        See Brown,
            Russell.
Ledru-Rollin,
        See Calman.
Lemaître, Jules,
        See Bishop.
Leopardi, Giacomo,
        See Van Horne.
Lesage, Alain-René,
        See Pierson.
Letourneur, Pierre,
        See Cushing.
Loisy, Alfred,
        See Lacombe.
Longfellow,
        See Goggio,
            Whitman.
Lope de Vega Carpio,
        See Brooks,
            Fichter,
            Phillips.
López de Ayala,
        See Kuersteiner.
Lulio, Raimundo,
        See Frost.
Machiavelli,
        See Di Santo.
Maistre, Joseph de,
        See Haines.

Maestro Herman el Alemán,
        See Smith.
Malebranche,
        See Doxsee.
Marguerite de Navarre,
        See Lamb,
            Walker.
Marie de France,
        See Jenkins.
Marino Jonata, Agnonese,
        See Ettari.
Maupassant,
        See Riddell.
Mesonero Romanos, Ramón de,
        See Berkowitz.
Michelet,
        See Pugh.
Mira de Amescua (*Antonio*),
        See Anibal,
            Buchanan.
Mistral, Frédéric,
        See Downer,
            Ford.
Molière,
        See Gadsby,
            Lorenz,
            Morley,
            Peirce.
Montalván, Juan Pérez de,
        See Bacon.
Montesquieu,
        See Dargan.
Navarro Villoslada, Francisco,
        See Cornish.
Nicole de Margival,
        See Todd.
Nodier, Charles,
        See Schenck.
Ovid,
        See Guyer,
            Jodocius.
Ortiz (*Agustín*),
        See House.
Païens de Maisières,
        See Hill.
Pascal,
        See The Linton sisters.

Péguy, Charles,
See Fialon.
Petrarch,
See McCabe,
Phelps.
Plato,
See Kerr,
Merrill.
Plautus,
See Rougier.
Poe, Edgar Allan,
See Cambiaire.
Pradon,
See Bussom.
Prévost, l'abbé
See Havens.
Pulci, Luigi,
See Shulters.
Quevedo,
See Rose.
Quinault, Philippe,
See Long.
Rabelais,
See Clement.
Racine,
See Canfield.
Renan,
See Brauer.
Ristoro d'Arezzo,
See Austin.
Rocaberti, Fra,
See Heaton.
Ronsard,
See Evers,
Storer.
Rosmini, Trentin Antonio,
See Bruno.
Rostand,
See Ross.
Rousseau,
See Foster,
Heller,
Peoples,
Staley,
Underwood.
Rymer, Thomas,
See Dutton.
Saint-Pierre, Abbé de,
See Ware.

Saint-Réal, l'abbé de,
See Happel.
Sainte-Beuve,
See Mac Clintock.
Salas Barbadillo, Alonso Ge-
rónimo,
See Place.
Sand, George,
See Schutz,
Staley.
Santillana, Marqués de,
See Seronde.
Scarron,
See Leavitt.
Scott, Walter,
See François,
Garnand.
Scribe, Eugène,
See Arvin.
Sedaine,
See Waterhouse.
Shakespeare,
See Boecker,
Gilman,
Wales.
Solís, Antonio de,
See Martell.
Spenser,
See McMurphy.
Staël, Mme. de,
See Jaeck,
Underwood.
Suárez de Figueroa, Cristó-
bal,
See Crawford.
Tacite,
See Delamarre.
Terence,
See Gadsby.
Thorndike's "The Teacher's
Work Book",
See Eddy.
Urfé, Honoré d',
See Fischer,
McMahon (Sister).
Végèce,
See Gebert.

Vergil,
　　See Naylor,
　　　　Storer.
Vigny, Alfred de,
　　See François,
　　　　Lebert.
Villehardouin,
　　See O'Connor.
Villemain,
　　See Atkin.
Villon,
　　See Neuenschwander.
Voltaire,
　　See Bruce,
　　　　Dulac,

Neuenschwander,
Pflueger,
Price,
Torrey,
White.

Wace,
　　See Crawford,
　　　　Hopkins.
Zabalete (or *Zavaleta*), *Juan de,*
　　See Doty.
Zayas y Sotomayor, María de,
　　See Place,
　　　　Sylvania.

COLUMBIA UNIVERSITY PRESS
Columbia University
New York

FOREIGN AGENT
OXFORD UNIVERSITY PRESS
HUMPHREY MILFORD
Amen House, London, E. C.

CARRANZA & CO., INC., NEW YORK

INSTITUT DES ÉTUDES FRANÇAISES

EDITOR

G. L. van Roosbroeck

ADVISORY BOARD

J. L. Gerig	R. Vaillant
H. Muller	R. M. Merrill
I. Brown	P. de La Rochelle

P. R. Sisson

PUBLICATIONS

Bei Fragen zur Produktsicherheit wenden Sie sich bitte an:
If you have any questions regarding product safety,
please contact:

Walter de Gruyter GmbH
Genthiner Straße 13
10785 Berlin
productsafety@degruyterbrill.com